Plato's *Euthyphro*

The Trial of Meletus

Translation and Commentary

Plato's *Euthyphro*

The Trial of Meletus

Translation and Commentary

Jeffrey C. Kalb, Jr.

Cover: *The Fall of Icarus* (1731)
Bernard Picart (1673-1733)

ISBN: 979-8-9866262-0-8

Beatae Mariae Semper Virgini,
Mediatrici, Coredemptrici, et Advocatae

Table of Contents

The renovation of Catholic culture will surely benefit from a prudent retrieval of the ancient Greek and Roman classics. Sadly, the natural, if fallen, attitude of pre-Christian man has been reinterpreted in the negations of post-Christian modernity. The most pliable of classical authors, Plato has suffered most palpably. Today he has few defenders even among Catholic intellectuals of a traditional mindset. Yet one would do well to recall that the Church Fathers, wary as they were of philosophy, invariably judged Plato to be in better conformity with Catholic doctrine than Aristotle. Political, economic, and cultural decline intervened. In a subsequent age, while all but two of Plato's works remained unknown to the West, Saint Thomas Aquinas forged a theology grounded in the Fathers and Aristotle, a theology that still enjoys the unbroken favor of the Church, even in these times of neglect. However, Aquinas received from Aristotle little more than a digest and critique of Platonic doctrine, fitted to a framework at odds with Plato's own intuitions and presented in a terminology foreign to his intentions. Today, Plato is graciously excused for being the teacher of Aristotle, rather than his student. Yet Plato is more easily criticized than understood, and to explain his dialogues in their own terms, rather than Aristotle's, is a worthy endeavor. It is to preserve the intellectual, pedagogical, and literary value of works unique in human history.

Both the argument and the literary richness of Plato's *Euthyphro* are unappreciated. This failure calls for explanation. *Euthyphro* certainly suffers from the unwillingness of many commentators to ponder anything but literal meanings. Rational demonstration is but a part of reasonable discourse. Yet every literary device is banished from consideration by *Euthyphro*'s interpreters, who effect a complete separation between the form and meaning of the dialogue. Stripped of these props, the dialogue appears as a series of questions leading to no sure conclusion. Consequently, not a few consider *Euthyphro* to teach no positive doctrines at all, but only a method of investigation. While it is true that we lack immediate access to Plato's mind, we must nevertheless regulate our reading by a pious desire to understand the author through all the signs he left for us, the figurative no less than the literal. This is no mere academic question, but one of justice.

A further distortion of *Euthyphro* derives from the unfounded division of Plato's literary work into early, middle, and late periods. Professing to see in the dialogues a development of his doctrine of Ideas, some scholars have ordered them in date of composition not by an independent and verifiable historical reference, but by private understanding of content and meaning. Instead of resolving merely apparent contradictions, commentators posit a doctrine in flux, maintaining that an early dialogue, so called, need not cohere with a late one in either doctrine or literary exposition. Plato's dialogues are no longer the elegant fruit of a lifetime of contemplation, but signposts in a fitful process of discovery and reconsideration. Plato, it is said casually, had composed *Euthyphro* well before the mature features of his philosophy developed. This would be a harmless claim, were not the unproven division used in turn as established fact. The temporal division of works disguises misunderstanding as intellectual history, uncritically prejudicing subsequent readings. At both the doctrinal and literary level, the reader is encouraged to neglect relationships between dialogues or, still worse, to set dialogues against each other. Shorn of their connections to the totality of Plato's writings, short dialogues, including *Euthyphro*, are particularly baffling.

Consequently, although the question proposed in *Euthyphro* is manifestly that of holiness, one must not imagine that this topic can be so easily isolated from Plato's philosophy taken as a whole. Plato's literary output is in many respects holographic. As one changes the viewing angle of a hologram, so also the image changes, and in such a way as to reveal it in depth. Were one to cut the hologram in half, one would not obtain two halves of the original image, but rather two separate and similar images. What is lost by the scission is not a part of the image, but rather its clarity and depth. This process of separation, taken to its natural limit, results in an obscure and superficial image. This is so because each part of the image is dispersed throughout the hologram, and the image is thereafter formed by the interaction of the entire hologram with the light shining upon it. In like manner, Plato's philosophy informs the whole body of his dialogues, and, viewing them all together in the light of reason, one perceives a single doctrine of clarity and depth. As one turns an eye to each dialogue individually, one sees not so much a part of a whole as the same doctrine under a different aspect. Separated from Plato's other works, the meaning of a short dialogue becomes obscure but, as connections to other dialogues and literary antecedents are reestablished, an astonishingly clear and beautiful image of his doctrine reemerges.

Several levels of description operate simultaneously in Plato's *Euthyphro*. Time, setting, plot, characters, and the common meaning of speech can be assigned to the literal level. These, in short, lend an air of concreteness to a conversation of dubious historicity. The social level consists of mores, political circumstances, and personal relations not always explicit in the text, but subject to Plato's critique. The philosophical level encompasses metaphysics, epistemology, and all things ancillary to wisdom. These three levels often intersect in a single term. For example, literally speaking, a god in *Euthyphro* is one of those immortal and superhuman characters found in Greek mythology; at the social level is understood the philosopher, deified by his vision of the Ideas; at the philosophical level, a god is the Idea itself. Consequently, when Socrates and Euthyphro speak of gods, one must consider implications at all three levels.

Claims that Plato possessed an esoteric doctrine likely derive from the figures and types through which his doctrine is expressed. Their consistency across so many works suggests a terminology adopted within his inner circle but easily passed over or misunderstood by the public. One ought to take seriously the observation, nay, admonition, put into the mouth of Alcibiades:

> If someone were to listen to the arguments of Socrates, the discourses would at first appear quite ridiculous, for on the outside they are covered over with names and phrases of that sort, the hide of a wanton satyr. For he speaks of pack-asses, of smiths, of shoemakers, and of tanners, and he always seems to say the same things by them, so that the inexperienced and unthinking person would ridicule his arguments in every respect. But, when they are opened, anyone entering within, seeing them afresh, will first find that they are the only discourses having any intelligence in them and, subsequently, that they contain matters most divine and a great many glorious images of virtue, aiming at everything that the man destined to be beautiful and good ought to examine. (*Symposium* 221e-222a)

The language of the marketplace and gymnasium, the casual and unexplored references, the jests and jibes, all are made to serve high intellectual purposes. The excavation of these figures from the text is well worth the labor and not always as difficult as may be thought.

Philology has no systematic precedence over philosophy, for every translator is a subtle but potent commentator. This is especially so when translating an expression of Plato, significations of which often lie below the surface of the text. Rendering an expression in English idiom will make the superficial meaning more accessible, but at the expense of the deeper associations that Plato certainly wished his Greek readers to make. Interpretation is effectively thwarted by translations that obscure literary antecedents, links to other dialogues, and the common roots of words, especially when translations come from the hands of different translators. Preserving these connections in English demands a consistent rendering of terms used by Plato with nuance, and this in turn demands the proper elasticity of an English equivalent, which is often problematic. Should this English translation of *Euthyphro* be deemed awkward or uncouth, some part of this can be attributed to the attempt to satisfy these requirements; the balance should be faulted to the translator. The translation in its entirety is presented in advance of the commentary, that those who are unfamiliar with the dialogue, or those who need to be refreshed about its content, may read it as an uninterrupted whole. The sole motive for this new translation is to supply English readers with a text that can bear a heavier weight of commentary than any previously available. Lack of polish will be repaired through philosophy.

Citation is simultaneously a justice to the labor of others and an aid to further investigation, but it too often degenerates into a grasping for credentials and the worship of received opinion. It would be a waste of the reader's limited time to repeat what one may easily find in other *Euthyphro* commentaries, none of which had any influence or bearing upon the present investigation. Nor would a sustained polemical stance toward those same commentaries further the study of Plato's doctrine or works. Extant translations have been preferred here for literary antecedents: David Grene's *Oedipus the King*, A. T. Murray's *Odyssey*, and Hugh G. Evelyn-White's *Theogony* and *Homeric Hymns*. For the reader's benefit, and as an acknowledgment of a benefit already received, know that much of the impetus and method of the present inquiry grew out of Jacob Klein's commentaries on *Meno* and *Phaedo*. Anyone who has an abiding interest in Plato can profit by these.

Euthyphro is both a profound meditation and a literary masterpiece meriting an honored place among the works of its author. It is no clumsy creature of Plato, but rather the victim of indelicate handling. Moreover, its elegant metaphysical solution to the critique of participation found in *Parmenides* proves the hypothesis of composition periods to be empty wind. Indeed, despite its brevity, *Euthyphro* has connections to most of Plato's dialogues. The ancients thought it prudent to practice upon a small work before commencing a larger one. Though rich in meaning, *Euthyphro* is a marvel of concision, a dialogue well suited to a much-needed reevaluation of Plato's doctrine and its literary expression.

Jeffrey C. Kalb, Jr.
Phoenix, Arizona
August 2022

Euthyphro: What novelty, Socrates, has come to pass that, having left behind your way of life in the Lyceum, you now wear away the time here around the Portico of the King Archon? For you surely do not have a suit before the King, as I have.

Socrates: The Athenians for their part, Euthyphro, are not calling it a private suit, but a public indictment.

Euthyphro: What are you saying? So, someone, it would seem, has brought an indictment against you? For I shall not charge this, at least, that you indicted the other man.

Socrates: Surely not.

Euthyphro: But another you?

Socrates: Very much so.

Euthyphro: Who is he?

Socrates: Well, I myself scarcely know the man, Euthyphro. For he seems to me to be someone young and unknown. But they call him Meletus, I think. And he is of the deme of Pitthus, if you should have in mind any Pitthean Meletus, the straight-haired sort, not very well bearded, but with a hooked nose.

Euthyphro: I have no one in mind, Socrates. But what kind of indictment has he brought against you?

Socrates: What kind? No low-born one, it seems to me. For to have come to know so great a matter is no paltry thing for one who is young. For he knows, so he says, in what manner the youth are corrupted and who they are who corrupt them. Perchance he is some wise man, and, looking down upon my lack of learnedness and seeing that I corrupt his peers, he comes to the state, as to a mother, accusing me. And he appears to me alone of the public men to begin rightly. For the right way is to take care of the young ones first in order that they may be as good as possible, just as a good farmer likely takes care of the young sprouts first, but after that the others also. And so Meletus, perhaps, is first weeding out those of us who corrupt the shoots of the young, as he says. Then after that, having cared for the older men, he will clearly become the cause of a multitude of the greatest goods for the city. At least, that would be the likely outcome to one beginning from such a beginning.

Euthyphro: I would wish it so, Socrates, but I fear that the opposite may happen. For, in undertaking to wrong you, he seems to me to begin an artless work of evil against the city, starting from the hearth. But tell me, what does he say you do to corrupt the young?

Socrates: Outlandish things, wondrous man, at least to hear it in this way. For he says that I am a maker of gods, and, for making fresh gods and not recognizing the ancient ones, he has brought an indictment against me on behalf of the latter, or so he says.

Euthyphro: I am beginning to understand, Socrates. It is no doubt because you say that a spirit visits you from time to time. He has therefore brought this indictment against you for making innovations about divine matters, and he comes into the court slandering, knowing that such things are easily received by the multitude. Why, they even ridicule me as a madman whenever I say something in the assembly concerning divine matters, foretelling to them things that will be. And yet not one of the things I have foretold is untrue. All the same, they are jealous of all people such as ourselves. Do not allow your understanding to be occupied with them, but rather come to close quarters with them.

Socrates: But, Euthyphro, my friend, perhaps their ridicule is of no matter. For it is of no violent concern to the Athenians if they consider someone to be clever, at least it seems to me, provided he is not fit to teach his wisdom. But whenever they think he makes others to be such a sort as well, they become angry, either from envy, as you say, or on account of something else.

Euthyphro: Well, I have no great wish to test exactly how they regard me in this.

Socrates: Indeed, and you appear, perhaps, to make yourself scarce, being unwilling to teach your own wisdom. But since I am a friend of mankind, I fear that I appear to pour out in speech to every man whatever I may possess, not only without a fee, but I would even gladly pay a fee if someone wanted to listen to me. So, if, as I was just saying, they were to ridicule me, as you say of yourself, it would not be unpleasant to pass the time playing like children and laughing in the court. But if they are in haste, how this will turn out is unclear, except to you prophets.

Euthyphro: Well, Socrates, perhaps the matter will come to nothing, and you will carry the case in accordance with your own mind, as I think that I shall also carry my own.

Socrates: And what is your suit, Euthyphro? Are you fleeing (defending) or pursuing (prosecuting)?

Euthyphro: I am pursuing.

Socrates: Whom?

Euthyphro: Someone I would seem mad to pursue.

Socrates: But why? Are you pursuing someone on the wing?

Euthyphro: He lacks much to fly, since he happens to be exceedingly old.

Socrates: Who is he?

Euthyphro: My father.

Socrates: Your own father, best of men?

Euthyphro: Most certainly.

Socrates: But what is the charge, and what does the suit concern?

Euthyphro: Murder, Socrates.

Socrates: Heracles! I suppose, Euthyphro, that the multitude does not know where the right lies. For I do not think it the part of just anyone to do it rightly, but only of the one driving wisdom somewhere very far.

Euthyphro: By Zeus, very far indeed, Socrates.

Socrates: But was the person killed by your father one of your relatives? But of course! For surely you would not charge him with murder for the sake of a stranger.

Euthyphro: It is ridiculous, Socrates, that you think it differs whether the man who was killed was a stranger or belonged to the household, whereas this alone must be safeguarded, whether the slayer slew in justice and if in justice, to allow it, but if not, to begin proceedings, even if the murderer is of a common hearth with you and shares a common table. For an equal pollution takes place if you knowingly associate with such a man, and do not purify both yourself and him by bringing suit. Now the man who was slain was a certain hireling of mine, and as we were farming on Naxos, he was laboring there with us. At any rate, having become drunk and angry with a certain one of our house-slaves, he cut his throat. My father then bound his hands and feet, throwing him into a certain ditch, and sent a man here to inquire from the interpreter of the law what he ought to do. But during this time, he esteemed him little and did not even care for the bound man, since he was a murderer, and it was therefore no matter if he should die, which very thing in fact happened; for he died of hunger and cold and the bonds before the messenger returned from the interpreter. Now my father and my other relatives are enraged about these things, because for the sake of this manslayer I am prosecuting for murder my own father, a man who either did not commit murder, as they say, or, if it were true that he killed him, since the man who was killed was himself a murderer, one need not take thought of such a one; for it is an unholy thing for a son to prosecute his father for murder. See how badly they know, Socrates, how the divine order holds concerning the holy and the unholy!

Socrates: But, in the name of Zeus, Euthyphro, do you think that you possess so accurate a knowledge concerning divine matters, of both holy and unholy things, that, when things have been done in the way you have described, you do not fear that by prosecuting your father you in turn may chance to perform an unholy deed?

Euthyphro: There would be no use for me, Socrates, nor would Euthyphro differ at all from the multitude of men, if I did not know accurately all such matters.

Socrates: Then the most excellent thing for me, wondrous Euthyphro, is to become your student, and, before the indictment, the one touching upon Meletus, to challenge him on these same things, saying that I for my part also in times past highly valued the knowledge of divinity, and that, since he says that I improvise rashly and miss the mark by innovating about divine things, I have now become your student. "And if, Meletus," I would say, "you agree that Euthyphro is wise about such matters, believe that I also acknowledge them rightly, and drop the charges. But if not, bring a charge against him, my teacher, rather than against me, for corrupting old men, both myself and his father, by teaching me and by correcting and punishing his father." And if I cannot persuade him either to drop the charge, or indict you instead of me, I could say the same things in the court that I was challenging him with.

Euthyphro: By Zeus, Socrates, if he should attempt to indict me, I think I would find where his weakness lies, and the argument in the court would come to be about him much sooner than about me.

Socrates: And consequently, my friend and companion, perceiving these things, I want to become your student, knowing that neither this Meletus nor anyone else seems to notice you at all. But so keenly and so easily has he observed me that he has indicted me for impiety. So now, in the name of Zeus, tell me what you just now claimed to know so clearly. What sort of thing do you say that the pious and the impious are, concerning both murder and other things? Is not the holy itself the self-same in every action, and is not the unholy itself, the opposite of everything holy, in turn, the self-same? And whatever the unholy is to be, will it not possess a single complete idea?

Euthyphro: Absolutely, Socrates.

Socrates: Tell me then, what do you say the holy and unholy are?

Euthyphro: Well now, I say that the holy is that which I am doing now: prosecuting a man who acts unjustly, missing the mark concerning either murder, or theft from temples, or any other such thing, whether it happens to be your father, or your mother, or anyone else. But not prosecuting is the unholy. Why, Socrates, see the great and sure sign I offer to you, one that I have described to others as well, that the law is so, and that if things happen thus, then rightly so, and moreover that one must not indulge the man who acts impiously, whoever he may be. For men acknowledge that Zeus is the best of the gods, and the most just, and yet they agree that he bound his father because the latter was unjustly swallowing his sons, and that his father, in turn, castrated his own father for other such things. But they are enraged against me, because I proceed against my father, who acts unjustly, and thus they say opposite things about the gods and about me.

Socrates: Is it not for this reason, Euthyphro, that I am fleeing the indictment, namely, that whenever someone says such things about the gods, I somehow find it hard to accept, because of which, it would seem, someone will say that I missed the mark. Now then, if these things seem true to you, who know so well about such things, it is surely necessary, so it would seem, that we also yield. For what shall we say, we who agree that we know nothing concerning these things? So, tell me, in the name of Zeus, the god of friendship, do you truly believe that these things happened so?

Euthyphro: Yes, Socrates, and things to be wondered at more than these, which the multitude does not know.

Socrates: And you believe that there was really a war amongst the gods, and terrible hatreds, and battles, and many other such things, the sort told by the poets and with which the temples have been adorned in many colors by good painters—but above all the robe that is carried up to the Acropolis during the festival of the Great Panathenaea is filled with such embroideries. Shall we say that these things are true, Euthyphro?

Euthyphro: Not only those, Socrates, but, as I was just saying, if you wish, I will detail for you many other things concerning divine matters, things I know you will be shocked to hear.

Socrates: I would not wonder at it. But you can tell me those things some other time at leisure. Right now, try to state more clearly that which I was in fact just asking you. For you did not, my comrade, sufficiently teach me before, when I was asking about the holy, as to what it may be, but you were telling me that this thing which you are now doing happens to be holy, namely, prosecuting your father for murder.

Euthyphro: And I was speaking the truth, Socrates.

Socrates: Perhaps. But you say, Euthyphro, that many other things are also holy.

Euthyphro: For they are.

Socrates: Do you remember then that I was not asking you to teach me one or two of the many holy things, but that very aspect by which all holy things are holy? For you said that it is by one idea that unholy things are unholy, and holy things holy. Do you not remember?

Euthyphro: I do.

Socrates: So then teach me now this idea, whatever it is, in order that I may look only to it, using it as a model by which, whenever you or anyone else does such a thing, I may say that it is holy, but if not such a thing, may deny it.

Euthyphro: Well, if you wish it in this way, Socrates, then I will say it in this way.

Socrates: Indeed, I do wish it.

Euthyphro: Well now, that which is beloved of the gods is holy, but that which is not beloved is unholy.

Socrates: You have now answered beautifully, and just as I was requiring you to answer. However, I do not yet know if this is true, but, clearly, you will go on and teach in full that the things you say are true.

Euthyphro: Surely.

Socrates: Carry on then. Let us examine what we are saying. The god-beloved thing and the god-beloved person are holy, but the god-hated thing and the god-hated person are unholy. They are not the same, but the holy is most opposite to the unholy. Is it not so?

Euthyphro: It is just so.

Socrates: And this seems to be stated well?

Euthyphro: I think so, Socrates.

Socrates: Well then, has this also been said, that the gods quarrel and differ with each other and that there are enmities in them for each other? Has this also been said?

Euthyphro: It has been said.

Socrates: And concerning what things, best of men, do disagreements produce enmity and rage? Let us examine it in this way. If you and I were to differ concerning number, as to which one was more, would these differences make us enemies and cause us to rage against each other, or rather, by resorting to counting in such matters, would we not be quickly reconciled?

Euthyphro: Certainly.

Socrates: And so, therefore, if we were to disagree concerning the greater and lesser, would we put an end to the disagreement by resorting to measurement?

Euthyphro: It is just so.

Socrates: And, by recourse to weighing, I think, we would settle our dispute concerning the heavier and lighter.

Euthyphro: How otherwise?

Socrates: But having differed about what, being unable to come to any judgment, would we be enemies and rage against each other? Perhaps the answer is not really at hand for you. But, as I speak, see if these things are the just and unjust, the beautiful and shameful, and the good and evil. Are not these the things about which, having differed and being yet unable to come to a satisfactory judgment, we become enemies to each other, when we do in fact become enemies, both you, and I, and all other men?

Euthyphro: Yes, these are the differences, Socrates. It concerns these things.

Socrates: Well? Would not the gods, Euthyphro, if in fact they do differ, differ on account of these things?

Euthyphro: It is a great necessity.

Socrates: And so, noble-born Euthyphro, according to your argument, some of the gods think that some things are just and unjust, and beautiful and shameful, and good and evil, but others think otherwise; for they would not in any way be quarreling with each other if they did not differ concerning these things? Is it so?

Euthyphro: You speak correctly.

Socrates: Therefore, the things which each group thinks are in fact beautiful and good and just, these things they love, but the things opposite to these they hate?

Euthyphro: Certainly.

Socrates: But these things, as you say, some think just, but others unjust. And disputing about these things they quarrel and wage war against each other. Is it not so?

Euthyphro: It is so.

Socrates: Then the same things, it would seem, are hated and loved by the gods, and the god-hated and god-beloved would be the same.

Euthyphro: It would seem so.

Socrates: And then holy things and unholy things would be the same, Euthyphro, by this argument.

Euthyphro: There is that possibility.

Socrates: Then you did not answer what I was asking, wondrous man. For I did not ask what one thing happens to be both holy and unholy, but it would seem that what is god-beloved is also god-hated. The result, Euthyphro, is that, with regard to what you are now doing, punishing your father, it would not be wondered at if doing this makes you beloved of Zeus, but an enemy to Cronos and Uranus, and beloved of Hephaestus, but an enemy to Hera. And if any one of the gods differs with another about the same, it will be the same for them too.

Euthyphro: But I think, Socrates, that concerning this at least, namely, that he who kills someone unjustly ought not to pay the penalty, not one of the gods differs, the one with the other.

Socrates: Well? Of men at least, Euthyphro, have you ever heard of anyone disputing that he who had killed unjustly, or had done anything else at all unjustly, ought not to pay the penalty?

Euthyphro: They never cease to dispute these things, both in the courts and elsewhere. For those who act unjustly in all such cases will say and do anything when fleeing a charge.

Socrates: But do they agree, Euthyphro, that they act unjustly and, thus agreeing, nevertheless say that they ought not to pay the penalty?

Euthyphro: In no way do they say that!

Socrates: Then, at least, they do not do and say everything. For I think they do not dare to say or dispute, that if they in fact act unjustly, the penalty need not be paid; but I think they deny that they act unjustly. Is it not so?

Euthyphro: You speak the truth.

Socrates: Then they do not, at least, dispute that the one acting unjustly ought not to pay the penalty. But perhaps they dispute about who is the one acting unjustly, and what he has done, and when.

Euthyphro: True indeed.

Socrates: Then even the gods have suffered the same, if in fact they quarrel concerning things just and unjust, as is your argument, and some affirm that others have acted unjustly, but some deny it? Since surely, wondrous man, no one, either of the gods or of men, dares to say that the penalty need not be paid by the one acting unjustly.

Euthyphro: Yes. You speak the truth, Socrates, in the main.

Socrates: But I think, Euthyphro, that the ones disputing, both gods and men, if in fact the gods do dispute, dispute each of the things that have been done. Differing about a certain action, some say that it has been done justly, but others say unjustly. Is it not so?

Euthyphro: Certainly.

Socrates: Come now, Euthyphro, my friend, teach me also, in order that I may become wiser, what evidence you have that all the gods think that the man was killed unjustly, who, being guilty of manslaughter while acting as a laborer, and having been bound by the master of the man who was killed, died on account of the bonds before he who bound him learned by inquiring of the legal interpreters what he must do about the matter, and, moreover, that for the sake of such a man it really is right that the son proceed against his father, prosecuting him for murder. Come, try to show me clearly about this, that all the gods think more than anything that it is right to do this. And if you show it sufficiently to me, I will never cease to praise you for your wisdom.

Euthyphro: But perhaps it is not a small task, Socrates, although certainly I could show it to you clearly.

Socrates: I am beginning to understand. It is because I seem to you less able to learn than the jurors; since it is clear that you will show them that these things are unjust and that all the gods together hate such things.

Euthyphro: Very clearly, Socrates, if they do indeed listen to me speak.

Socrates: But they will listen, so long as you seem to speak well. But I thought this while you were speaking, and I am considering it with regard to myself. If Euthyphro were to teach me that all the gods think that such a death is unjust, what more have I learned from Euthyphro, as to what the holy and the unholy are? For this work, so it seems, would be god-hated. But just now it was shown that the holy and what is not holy are not defined in this way; for that which is god-beloved appeared to be also that which is god-hated, with the result that I let you off from this, Euthyphro. If you wish, let all the gods think it unjust and hate it. Shall we now amend the definition, that whatever all the gods hate is unholy and whatever they all love is holy, but what some love and others hate is neither or both? Do you wish to define the holy and the unholy in this way now?

Euthyphro: For what hinders, Socrates?

Socrates: Nothing on my part, Euthyphro, but examine your own, whether in thus proposing it you will easily teach me what you promised.

Euthyphro: Well, I would say that this is the holy, namely, that which all the gods love, and the opposite, that which all the gods hate, is the unholy.

Socrates: Shall we therefore, Euthyphro, examine again whether this is beautifully said, or shall we let it be, and accept it in this way, from both ourselves and others, if someone were merely to assert that the matter stands thus, conceding that it does? Must what the speaker says be examined?

Euthyphro: It must be examined. Yet I for my part think that it has now been defined beautifully.

Socrates: Good man, we shall soon know better, for I had in mind such a thing: Is the holy loved by the gods because it is holy, or is it holy because it is loved?

Euthyphro: I don't know what you mean, Socrates.

Socrates: Then I shall try to speak more clearly. We say that there is something being carried and something carrying, something being led and something leading, something being seen and something seeing. Do you begin to understand with regard to all such things that they do differ from each other, and in what manner they differ?

Euthyphro: I am beginning to understand, or at least it seems to me.

Socrates: There is also, therefore, something being loved, and the thing loving is other than this?

Euthyphro: How otherwise?

Socrates: Tell me now, whether the thing being carried is a thing being carried because it is carried, or on account of something else.

Euthyphro: No, on that account.

Socrates: And the thing being led because it is led, and the thing being seen because it is seen?

Euthyphro: Certainly.

Socrates: Not then because it is a thing being seen, on account of this is it seen, but conversely, because it is seen, on account of this a thing being seen; nor because it is a thing being led, on account of this is it led, but because it is led, on account of this a thing being led; nor because it is a thing being carried is it carried, but because it is carried, a thing being carried. Is that which I wish to say becoming clearer, Euthyphro? I wish to say this: that if something is generated or undergoes something, not because it is a thing being generated is it generated, but because it is generated, it is a thing being generated; nor because it is a thing undergoing, does it undergo, but because it undergoes it is a thing undergoing; or do you not agree?

Euthyphro: I do agree.

Socrates: And so also the thing being loved is by this either something being generated or undergoing something?

Euthyphro: Certainly.

Socrates: And does this hold in the same way the previous cases do? Not because it is a thing being loved is it loved by those by whom it is loved, but because it is loved it is a thing being loved.

Euthyphro: Necessarily.

Socrates: What then do we say concerning the holy, Euthyphro? Is it loved by all the gods according to your argument?

Euthyphro: Yes.

Socrates: On account of this, that it is a holy thing, or on account of something else?

Euthyphro: No, but on account of this.

Socrates: It is loved because it is a holy thing; not because it is loved, on account of this is it a holy thing?

Euthyphro: It would seem so.

Socrates: But the god-beloved is the god-beloved and a thing being loved because it is loved by the gods.

Euthyphro: How otherwise?

Socrates: Then the god-beloved is not the holy, Euthyphro, nor is the holy the god-beloved, as you say, but the former differs from the latter in this respect.

Euthyphro: How so, Socrates?

Socrates: Because we agree that the holy is loved on account of this, that it is holy, but it is not holy because it is loved. Do we not?

Euthyphro: Yes.

Socrates: But we agree that the god-beloved, because it is loved by the gods, is, by this very passion of being loved, god-beloved, but not because it is god-beloved, on account of this is it loved.

Euthyphro: Truly spoken.

Socrates: But if, my friend, Euthyphro, the god-beloved and the holy were the same thing, then if on the one hand the holy were loved on account of being holy, the god-beloved would also be loved on account of being the god-beloved, but if the god-beloved were the god-beloved on account of being loved by the gods, the holy would also be holy on account of being loved. But now you see that it holds conversely, and that the one is altogether different from the other. For the one has the character of being loved only because it is loved; but the other has the character of being loved, and only on account of this is it loved. And you run the risk, Euthyphro, when asked what the holy is, of not wishing to make clear to me its essence, but rather describing something which it has undergone, something the holy has suffered, specifically, to be loved by all the gods. But what it is you have not yet said. So, if this is something beloved of you, do not hide it away from me, but tell me again from the beginning: What is holiness, no matter if it is loved by the gods or if it undergoes something? Concerning this we shall not be set at odds, but speak straightforwardly, what are the holy and the unholy?

Euthyphro: But, Socrates, I for my part am unable to say to you what I have in mind. For whatever we propose to ourselves somehow goes about endlessly, not wanting to remain where we seat it.

Socrates: Euthyphro, your arguments would appear to belong to Daedalus, my ancestor. And if I were making them and laying them down, perhaps you would jest with me that on account of my kinship with him my works in words run away and do not wish to remain where one puts them. But now the suppositions are your own; there is need of some other jest. For they do not want to stay put for you, as is apparent even to yourself.

Euthyphro: But it seems to me that these definitions call for the joke well enough, Socrates, for I am not the one who has put into them this going about and not remaining, but you seem to me to be the Daedalus, since from my part these things would be staying put.

Socrates: Then, my companion, I have perhaps become more adept in the art than even that great man, inasmuch as he was making only his own works to not remain, but I both my own works, so it would seem, and those of another. What's more, this art of mine is most ingenious because I am wise against my will. For I would have wished my words to stay in place and be made to sit down motionless, more than to obtain the wisdom of Daedalus and the wealth of Tantalus. But enough of these things! Since you seem to me to fare languidly and sumptuously, I myself will be zealous in your behalf, that you may teach me about the holy. And do not give up too soon. For see if it does not seem necessary to you that everything holy is just.

Euthyphro: It does.

Socrates: Is then every just thing also holy, or every holy thing also just, or is not every just thing holy, but some part of the just holy and part of it something else?

Euthyphro: Socrates, I cannot follow your arguments.

Socrates: And yet you are younger than I by as much as you are the wiser. But, as I say, you fare luxuriantly because of your wealth of wisdom. But, blessed man, strain yourself. For to apprehend what I am saying is not difficult. For I am saying the reverse of what the poet said, he who wrote: "But Zeus, who performed these works, planting all these things, do not crave to name. For where there is fear, there also is reverence." Now I differ with this poet. Shall I tell you in what way.

Euthyphro: Certainly.

Socrates: It does not seem to me that where there is fear there is also reverence. For many men fearful of diseases and poverty and many other such things seem to me to fear, but do not revere in any way these things which they fear. Does it not also seem so to you?

Euthyphro: Certainly.

Socrates: Rather, where there is reverence, there is also fear, for is there anyone who, feeling reverence, is ashamed of some deed, but has not at the same time dreaded or feared the reputation of baseness?

Euthyphro: Indeed, he would fear it.

Socrates: Then it is not right to say "for where there is fear, there also is reverence," but rather, "where there is reverence, there also is fear." For reverence is not everywhere fear is, since fear, I think, is something larger than reverence. For reverence is but a part of fear, just as the odd is a part of number, with the result that the odd is not everywhere number is, but rather, number is everywhere the odd is. Perhaps you follow now?

Euthyphro: Certainly.

Socrates: It was such a thing I meant before in asking whether where the just is, the holy is also there, or, where the holy is, there also is the just, but the holy is not everywhere the just is; for the holy is a part of the just. Shall we speak in this way or does it seem otherwise to you.

Euthyphro: No, but in this way. For you seem to me to speak rightly.

Socrates: Now look at what comes next. For if the holy is a part of the just, it is necessary, it would seem, that we find out what sort of part of the just the holy is. If you asked me about some one of the things just discussed, for example, what part of number the even is and what this number happens to be, I would say, "that which has not unequal, but equal divisions." Or does it not seem so to you?

Euthyphro: It does to me.

Socrates: Try now to teach me in this way what part of the just the holy is, in order that we may also tell Meletus to no longer wrong us or indict us for impiety, since I have sufficiently learned from you the things that are pious and holy and those that are not.

Euthyphro: It seems to me, Socrates, that the part of the just concerning the tending of the gods is pious and holy, but that the remaining part of the just is that concerning men.

Socrates: You appear to me to speak beautifully, Euthyphro. But I am still lacking one little thing. For I do not yet understand what sort of thing you call "tending". For you surely do not mean the same sort of tending of the gods as of other things. For we mean, indeed we affirm, that not everyone knows how to tend horses, but the horse-trainer does. Is it so?

Euthyphro: Certainly.

Socrates: For I suppose the art of horse training is the tending of horses.

Euthyphro: Yes.

Socrates: Nor does everyone know how to tend dogs, but the hunter does?

Euthyphro: It is so.

Socrates: For I suppose the art of hunting is the tending of dogs.

Euthyphro: Yes.

Socrates: And the art of the oxherd is the tending of oxen?

Euthyphro: Certainly.

Socrates: And the art of holiness and piety is the tending of the gods, Euthyphro? Do you mean this?

Euthyphro: I do.

Socrates: Now does tending always accomplish the same thing? I mean such as this: Is it for the good and benefit of the one being tended, as indeed you see that horses that are tended by the horse trainer are benefited and become better? Do they not seem so to you?

Euthyphro: To me they do.

Socrates: And dogs somehow by the hunter's art and oxen by the oxherd's art, and all other things in the same way? Or do you think that tending is for the harm of the one being tended?

Euthyphro: By Zeus, not I!

Socrates: But for its benefit?

Euthyphro: How otherwise?

Socrates: Then holiness, being the tending of the gods, is a benefit to the gods and makes the gods better? And would you agree that whenever you do something holy you are making some one of the gods better?

Euthyphro: By Zeus, not I!

Socrates: Nor, Euthyphro, do I think that you mean this, and far from it! But I was asking for the sake of this, what you might mean by tending of the gods, not in fact thinking that you mean such a thing.

Euthyphro: And rightly so, Socrates. For I do not mean such a thing.

Socrates: Be it so. But what tending of the gods would holiness be?

Euthyphro: That, Socrates, which slaves tend to their masters.

Socrates: I am beginning to understand. It would be, so it would seem, some service to the gods.

Euthyphro: Very much so.

Socrates: Can you say then the service to doctors, for the accomplishment of what work is it a service? Do you not think it is for the sake of health?

Euthyphro: I do.

Socrates: Well, then? The service to shipbuilders, for the accomplishment of what work is it a service?

Euthyphro: Clearly, Socrates, for the construction of a ship.

Socrates: And the service to builders is for the construction of a house?

Euthyphro: Yes.

Socrates: Then do tell, best of men, this service to the gods, for the accomplishment of what work would it be a service? For it is clear that you know, since in fact you say that you know about divine things, at least, better than any other man.

Euthyphro: And I speak the truth, Socrates.

Socrates: Tell me then, in the name of Zeus, whatever could that all-beautiful work be, which the gods accomplish, employing us as servants?

Euthyphro: Many beautiful things, Socrates.

Socrates: Yes, and generals too, friend, but you might likewise easily say that the chief of these is that they attain victory in battle. Is it not so?

Euthyphro: How otherwise?

Socrates: And farmers accomplish many and, I think, beautiful things. But, likewise, the chief of these works is a brood out of the earth.

Euthyphro: Certainly.

Socrates: Well then? Of the many beautiful things that the gods accomplish, what is the chief work?

Euthyphro: I told you a little earlier, Socrates, that it is a rather great work to learn accurately how all these things stand. I simply say to you this, that if someone possesses the knowledge of doing and saying things pleasing to the gods by praying and sacrificing, these are holy things, and such things preserve both one's own house and the common interests of cities; but the opposites of these pleasing things are impious, and overturn and destroy everything together.

Socrates: If you wished, Euthyphro, you might have told me much more briefly the chief of the things I was asking about. But it is indeed clear that you are not prepared to teach me. For just now when you were upon it, you turned away, but if you had answered, I would have learned sufficiently from you about holiness. Now, however, it is necessary that the one asking follow the one being asked wherever he should lead. What then, once more, do you say that the holy and holiness are? Is it not some knowledge of sacrificing and praying?

Euthyphro: I think so.

Socrates: And is not then sacrificing the giving of gifts to the gods and is not praying a begging of the gods?

Euthyphro: Very much so, Socrates.

Socrates: Then according to this argument holiness would be a knowledge of begging and giving gifts.

Euthyphro: You understand beautifully, Socrates, what I was saying.

Socrates: For I am desirous, my friend, of your wisdom and put forth my mind to it, in order that whatever you say may not fall to the ground. But tell me, what is this service to the gods? Do you say that it is to beg from and give to them?

Euthyphro: I do.

Socrates: Would not then begging rightly be asking them for those things which we are lacking?

Euthyphro: But what else?

Socrates: And in turn giving rightly would be to present in return those things which they happen to lack from us? For it would not in any way be artful that the one bringing gifts should give to someone those things of which he has no lack.

Euthyphro: Truly spoken, Socrates.

Socrates: Then holiness, Euthyphro, would be a mercantile art for gods and men between each other.

Euthyphro: 'Mercantile' if it pleases you to name it thus.

Socrates: But it is no pleasure to me if it does not happen to be true. Now tell me, what benefit is there to the gods from the gifts that they receive from us? For the things that they give are clear to all. For we have nothing good which they do not in some way give. But how are they benefited by the things they receive from us? Or do we so far overreach them in bartering that we receive all good things from them, but they get nothing from us?

Euthyphro: But do you think, Socrates, that the gods are benefited by these things they receive from us?

Socrates: But whatever would these be, Euthyphro, the gifts from us to the gods?

Euthyphro: What else would it be than honor and recognition and, what I was just saying, gratitude?

Socrates: Is the holy then, Euthyphro, that which is grateful to the gods, but not that which is beneficial or beloved of the gods?

Euthyphro: I for my part think that it is beloved more than anything.

Socrates: Then it would seem that the holy is again the thing beloved of the gods.

Euthyphro: Yes, above all else.

Socrates: Saying these things, do you then wonder if your words appear not to remain still but to walk about, and will you allege as a cause myself, a Daedalus, of making them walk, while you are much more skillful than Daedalus and make them go about in a circle? Or do you not perceive that our argument has come round again to the same definition? For you remember, I suppose, that the holy and that which is god-beloved did not seem to us the same thing before, but different from each other. Or do you not remember?

Euthyphro: I do remember.

Socrates: Do you not comprehend now that you say that the thing beloved of the gods is holy? But is this something god-beloved or not?

Euthyphro: It is the same.

Socrates: Then either we were not agreeing beautifully before or, if beautifully then, we are not proposing rightly now.

Euthyphro: It would seem so.

Socrates: Then we must investigate again what the holy is, since I shall not willingly shrink from it out of cowardice before I learn. Do not despise me, but, applying your mind, by every means, tell me the truth fully now. For you know, if in fact any man does, and just like Proteus you must not be released until you speak. For, if you did not know clearly both the holy and the unholy, it is impossible that you would ever attempt to prosecute for murder an old man, your father, for the sake of a manservant, but you would have feared the gods to take such a risk, lest you should do it wrongfully and be shamed before men. But now I know well that you think you know clearly the holy and the unholy. Speak then, Euthyphro, best of men, and do not hide away what you think.

Euthyphro: Another time, Socrates. For I am now hastening somewhere, and it is time for me to depart.

Socrates: What a thing you are doing, companion! You have left me, casting me down from the great hope which I had that, having learned from you about both holy things and those that are not, I would be freed from Meletus's charge, showing to him that I have become wise from Euthyphro about divine matters, and that I no longer rashly improvise from ignorance, nor do I innovate concerning these same things, and above all that I shall live better the rest of my life.

Euthyphro Commentary

Even were this no matter of God's ordinance it would not fit you so to leave it lie, unpurified, since a good man is dead and one that was a king. Search it out.

Sophocles, *Oedipus the King,* 255-258

The Person of Euthyphro

Before entering upon an interpretation of *Euthyphro*, one ought to address the question of the historicity of both the eponymous character and the conversation that the dialogue purportedly describes. One should understand the literal meaning of his name, consider how the character of Euthyphro is employed in Plato's dialogues and weigh external historical references. "Euthyphro" is derived from εὐθύς, meaning "straight" or "direct," and φρόνημα, meaning "mind" or "thought." "Euthyphro" thus describes one whose mind gets straight to the essence of things. The irony of the name becomes clear as Euthyphro literally argues in circles in his attempt to define "holiness" for Socrates. The rather implausible coincidence required to create this irony argues against the historical existence of such a figure, making it more likely that Euthyphro was merely a stand-in for a real person whom Plato wished to criticize. As the historicity of the person goes, so also goes the conversation. Entering deeply into the dialogue, one will find so many useful literary coincidences that the content of the encounter could only be contrived. Diogenes Laertius reports:

> They say that Socrates, having heard Plato recite the latter's dialogue, *Lysis*, said, "Heracles! How many falsehoods this young man utters about me!" For the man had written not a few things which Socrates had never said. (*Lives of the Eminent Philosophers*, III.35)

The dialogues are not histories, but brilliant literary works composed to enact the author's doctrines in concrete settings, whether real or imagined.

Bearing in mind that Meletus, Socrates' primary accuser, made his accusations of atheism on behalf of the poets and their theogonies, one can easily recognize a suitable substitute in the character of Euthyphro, who appears indirectly in the humorous verbal gymnastics of Plato's *Cratylus*:

> **Hermogenes:** And indeed, Socrates, you appear to me to be pronouncing oracles suddenly and without art, just like those who are inspired.
>
> **Socrates:** Yes, Hermogenes, and for my part I allege that it descended upon me from Euthyphro of Prospalta. For I was with him from early morning and gave him an ear. So, he was probably inspired, and not only sailed into my ears with his supernatural wisdom but took hold of my soul as well. (*Cratylus* 396d)

That Euthyphro pronounces "oracles suddenly and without art" indicates that he prophesies without genuine knowledge. In *Cratylus* Socrates admits:

> With respect to "fire" (πῦρ) I am at a loss. The muse of Euthyphro has surely abandoned me, or else this is in all respects a difficult thing. (*Cratylus* 409d)

The "muse of Euthyphro" indicates that Euthyphro is, or at least claims to be, a poet, thus connecting him with Meletus and his charge against Socrates:

> From out of these [men] Meletus attacked me, and Anytus and Lycon, Meletus being vexed on behalf of the poets, Anytus for the artisans and statesmen, Lycon for the orators. (*Apology* 123e-24a)

There is one possible reference to an historical Euthyphro in the work of Diogenes Laertius, who mentions him in passing as he praised the capacities of Socrates:

> [Socrates] was sufficient in both respects, in both exhorting and dissuading: Having engaged in dialectic with Theaetetus about the nature of knowledge, he sent him away divinely inspired, as Plato tells it, but he drew Euthyphro away from his intention to indict his father for the murder of a stranger, after having examined dialectically with him the nature of holiness. (*Lives of the Eminent Philosophers*, VI.40)

Under close observation, however, the citation yields no extrinsic support for the existence of either Euthyphro or the conversation, since it provides nothing outside of what could have been gleaned from the dialogue itself. Short of such evidence, there is no way to prove that Euthyphro ever existed, while proving the opposite is of its very nature impossible, no matter how probable it may be. Nevertheless, one may, without committing to either the existence or non-existence of such a person, recognize the suitability of Euthyphro as a stand-in for Meletus, whom Socrates will put on trial according to his own standards and methods. This reversal becomes explicit in the dialogue itself.

The Setting and Its Associations

Euthyphro: *What novelty, Socrates, has come to pass that, having left behind your way of life in the Lyceum, you now wear away the time here around the Portico of the King Archon? For you surely do not have a suit before the King, as I have.*

Euthyphro is surprised to find Socrates at the Portico of the King Archon, a definite departure from the customary life of Socrates, who was wont to pass his time in the Lyceum investigating philosophical truths. For his part, Euthyphro is quite accustomed to passing his time in the courts, engaged in suits, not unlike Meletus, one may suppose. Yet Plato manages to endow this admission with a biting reproach through his expression about wearing away the time, for it is the precise language he uses in the *Republic* to discredit men who give themselves to this sort of life:

"Does it not seem shameful and a great and sure token of a lack of education to be compelled to use the justice brought in from others, as from masters and judges, while one dwells in perplexity?" "The most shameful of all things." "Or does this," I said, "seem to you to be more shameful still, when someone not only wears away the greater part of life defending and accusing in the courts of law, but, from ignorance of the beautiful, is persuaded to make a display of this very thing, showing himself a man clever in practicing injustice, twisting every turn, passing through every escape, averting every throw, in order that he may not submit to justice, and all for trivial and worthless things?" (*Republic* 405a-c)

Such men have no justice living within them but seek to apply a standard from without. They are ignorant of the beautiful life and, by implication, all that is necessary to lead it.

The King Archon[1], by then a partially defunct office, held responsibility primarily in religious matters, a point of importance in a dialogue that professes to investigate the nature of holiness and piety. The stranger in Plato's *Statesman* reminds us:

In many places among the Greeks, one would find the greatest sacrifices concerning things of this sort are assigned to the greatest offices. And what I say should be clearer to you [Athenians] than to all others, for they say that the most august and ancestral of the ancient sacrifices are performed by the King Archon, who is chosen by lot. (*Statesman* 290e)

The kingly portico at which Socrates and Euthyphro meet cannot fail to suggest Plato's doctrine that the kingly art ought to be practiced by the philosopher, most famously expressed in his seventh epistle:

In praising the correct philosophy, I was compelled to say that it is from this that all just things, both of states and of individuals, are surveyed. Therefore, the various classes of men will not rest from evils until either the class of those who philosophize rightly and in truth have come to political rule, or else the class of those who hold political power will, out of some divine allotment, genuinely philosophize. (*Epistle VII* 326a-b)

Plato also uses the setting to invoke some literary antecedents. First, the presence of the plainly, perhaps even shabbily, dressed Socrates in the Portico calls to mind Homer's literary hero, Odysseus. King Odysseus, after many years of warring and wandering, returns to his native Ithaca only to find that younger men are courting his wife, Penelope, and despoiling the state. Disguised as a beggar, he passes his time in the portico of his own palace, learning by observation who is friend and foe. Odysseus eventually slays his wife's suitors and reaffirms his own kingship. *Euthyphro* reenacts the famed contest of the stringing of the bow of Odysseus, with Socrates in the role of Odysseus and Euthyphro as Telemachus, his son. Socrates will indeed slay the suiters with his arguments.

However, even more common in *Euthyphro* is Plato's use of *Oedipus the King*, the renowned tragedy of Sophocles. This tragedy serves to generate analogies at a number of different levels. In keeping with the nature of Greek tragedy, *Oedipus the King* has but a single setting, in this case before the altars in front of the royal palace of Thebes. Unbeknownst to Oedipus, he has killed his father and married his mother. The tragedy consists in the gradual revelation to Oedipus of his true parentage and the moral standing of his actions, culminating in his own self-blinding after recognizing his deeds. As this dialogue develops, allusions to the impiety of Oedipus will elucidate the points that Plato is making.

Echoes of *Oedipus the King* are not unique to *Euthyphro*. Plato takes up this question of kingliness explicitly in his *Statesman*:

> **Stranger:** Well then, if someone, being himself a private citizen, is such a one as to advise a man who rules as king, shall we not say that he has the very knowledge that the ruler must have acquired?
>
> **Young Socrates:** We shall say this.
>
> **Stranger:** But the knowledge of the true king is the kingly knowledge?
>
> **Young Socrates:** Yes.
>
> **Stranger:** Then the man who has acquired this knowledge, whether he happens to be a ruler or a private citizen, will he not rightly, and wholly in accordance with the same art, be called kingly? (*Statesman* 259a-b)

This echoes Creon, who was accused by Oedipus of wanting the throne for himself. Creon answers in profoundly philosophical terms that cannot have been far from Plato's mind:

> Consider, first, if you think any one
> would choose to rule and fear rather than rule
> and sleep untroubled by a fear if power
> were equal in both cases. I, at least,
> I was not born with such a frantic yearning
> to be a king – but to do what kings do.
> And so it is with everyone who has learned
> wisdom and self-control. As it stands now,
> the prizes are all mine – and without fear.
> (*Oedipus the King*, 584-590)

It is the character of the man that makes him kingly, not the office that he holds. He "who has learned wisdom and self-control" has the power of acting as a king, whereas the actual officeholder may fall far short of kingliness.

The Charges Against Socrates

Socrates: *The Athenians for their part, Euthyphro, are not calling it a private suit, but a public indictment.*

Euthyphro: *What are you saying? So, someone, it would seem, has brought an indictment against you? For I shall not charge this, at least, that you indicted the other man.*

Socrates: *Surely not.*

Euthyphro: *But another you?*

Socrates: *Very much so.*

Plato makes several points in this exchange. First, through the mouth of Socrates, he calls into question whether the complaint against Socrates was genuinely a question for the whole state, or merely expressed a personal grudge against him. A suit (δική) was for the Athenians a legal action of a private matter, to be adjudicated between individuals or households; an indictment (γραφή) was, on the other hand, a matter that concerned the state directly.[2] Of a similar cast is the question posed by Menelaus to Telemachus in the *Odyssey*:

> Then he sat down beside Telemachus, and spoke, and addressed him: "What need has brought thee hither, prince Telemachus, to goodly Lacedaemon over the broad back of the sea? Is it a public matter, or thine own? Tell me the truth of this." (*Odyssey* 4.312-314)

Second, Plato reinforces the notion that Socrates would never engage in such legal wrangling as does his accuser. Third, and for the first time in the dialogue, he has set up a parallel between private and public morality, between the family and the state. This parallel becomes more explicit and important as the dialogue progresses.

It would be useful to recall another point of contact, for now merely implicit, between Meletus and Oedipus. In his rage, Oedipus does not seek the mere banishment of Creon. He wants to put him to death:

> **Creon:**   What do you want them to do then? Banish me?
>
> **Oedipus:**   No, certainly; kill you, not banish you. (*Oedipus the King,* 622-623)

Meletus, for wishing to put Socrates to death, is thus identified with Oedipus:

> **Creon:**   Were his eyes straight in his head? Was his mind right
>   when he accused me in this fashion?
>   (*Oedipus the King,* 528-529)

The mind of Meletus is indeed far from straight.

Meletus the Accuser

Euthyphro: *Who is he?*

Socrates: *Well, I myself scarcely know the man, Euthyphro. For he seems to me to be someone young and unknown. But they call him Meletus, I think. And he is of the deme of Pitthus, if you should have in mind any Pitthean Meletus, the straight-haired sort, not very well bearded, but with a hooked nose.*

Meletus is by no means a prominent Athenian. Socrates even professes to be a bit unsure about the name of the man who accuses him of corrupting the youth and spreading atheism. In this too Meletus is cast in the mold of Oedipus. Teiresias prophesies:

> In name he is a stranger among citizens
> but soon he will be shown to be a citizen
> true native Theban, and he'll have no joy
> of the discovery: blindness for sight
> and beggary for riches his exchange,
> he shall go journeying to a foreign country
> tapping his way before him with a stick.
> (*Oedipus the King*, 452-456)

Like Oedipus, Meletus sees only with his eyes. According to Diogenes Laertius, Meletus, this "stranger among citizens," was indeed cast out, having been executed after the Athenians felt remorse for the execution of Socrates. (*Lives of the Eminent Philosophers*, II.42)

The youth and inexperience of Meletus is made plain by the fact that his beard has not yet come in fully. As Pausanias notes in the *Symposium*, the acquisition of mind "draws near with the beginning of a beard." (*Symposium* 181d) One may surmise then that Plato wishes to emphasize Euthyphro's superficial education and understanding. Meletus comes from the Deme of Pitthus, which was named for Pittheus, son of Pelops, son of Tantalus. This may not appear important, but as identities are revealed by comparison with other dialogues, this lineage connects his education to Prodicus, the atheist. Finally, the hooked nose of Meletus suggests his sophistical education. The angler, or fisherman, and his hook are symbolic of the sophist:

Stranger: By the gods, have we not recognized that the one man is akin to the other?

Theaetetus: Who is akin to whom?

Stranger: The angler is akin to the sophist. (*Sophist*, 221d)

For contrast one should keep in mind the pug nose of Socrates.

Euthyphro: I have no one in mind, Socrates. But what kind of indictment has he brought against you?

Socrates: What kind? No low-born one, it seems to me. For to have come to know so great a matter is no paltry thing for one who is young. For he knows, so he says, in what manner the youth are corrupted and who they are who corrupt them. Perchance he is some wise man, and, looking down upon my lack of learnedness and seeing that I corrupt his peers, he comes to the state, as to a mother, accusing me.

It is quite common in Plato's dialogues that words are double-edged. Here, ἀμαθία, literally "lack of learnedness," has a second meaning and, as is also quite common, this meaning is established through the ridiculously implausible derivation of the word that Socrates makes in *Cratylus*:

for the former, ἀμαθία, seems to be "the progression of he who goes together with God" (τοῦ ἅμα θεῷ ἰόντος πορεία). (*Cratylus* 437b-c)

One should not underestimate the wealth of connotations Plato brings to the dialogue by this easily overlooked banter. Plato, in his dialogue on holiness, has by a single stroke already established Socrates as one who walks with God.

However, of even greater importance in this exchange is Plato's definitive analogy between the political body and the family. The analogy is also made in Plato's *Statesman*, in which the Stranger groups kingship, statesmanship, and household management under the same art:

Therefore, with regard to what we were just now discussing, it is apparent that there is a single knowledge concerning all these things, and whether someone calls it the knowledge of kingship, statesmanship, or household management, let us not differ with him in this. (*Statesman* 259c)

In *Euthyphro* Plato makes the analogy even more explicit: The king is the father; the state is the mother; the citizen is the son. Thus, the son (Meletus) has gone to his mother (the state) to accuse his king and father (Socrates). Indeed, democratic Athens, like Ithaca, suffers from a plenitude of suitors, each seeking to marry the mother (acquire political authority), all the while enriching themselves while the philosopher-king is absent:

Then wise Telemachus answered him: "Menelaus, son of Atreus, fostered by Zeus, leader of hosts, I came if haply thou mightest tell me some tidings of my father. My home is being devoured and my rich lands are ruined; with men that are foes my house is filled, who are ever slaying my thronging sheep and my sleek kine of shambling gait, even the wooers of my mother, overweening in their insolence. (*Odyssey* 4.315-321)

But wily Odysseus has returned in the form of Socrates, to bind these suitors of the state with "cords of destruction," that is, by his arguments: "So spoke each man, for verily they thought that he had not slain the man willfully; and in their folly they knew not this, that over themselves one and all the cords of destruction had been made fast." (*Odyssey* 22.31)

But even more important are the connections to *Oedipus the King*. Meletus seeks to take the political place that belongs to his genuine and kingly father, Socrates. He will kill his own father unknowingly, because, like Oedipus, he does not know who his parents are. As Teiresias spoke of Oedipus, so too may one speak of Meletus:

> He shall be proved father and brother both
> to his own children in his house; to her
> that gave him birth, a son and husband both;
> a fellow sower in his father's bed
> with that same father that he murdered.
> Go within, reckon that out, and if you find me
> mistaken, say I have no skill in prophecy.
> (*Oedipus the King*, 457-461)

Moreover, like Oedipus, Meletus is not simply a victim of circumstances. It is his hubris, his very lack of piety and holiness, that leads him to commit these crimes.

Education

... And he appears to me alone of the public men to begin rightly. For the right way is to take care of the young ones first in order that they may be as good as possible, just as a good farmer likely takes care of the young sprouts first, but after that the others also. And so Meletus, perhaps, is first weeding out those of us who corrupt the shoots of the young, as he says. Then after that, having cared for the older men, he will clearly become the cause of a multitude of the greatest goods for the city. At least, that would be the likely outcome to one beginning from such a beginning.

Meletus is truly a "sower in his father's bed," for education is immediately cast in agricultural terms. Through Socrates, Plato raises the question of who should be educated first and how. Socrates proposes that it is the youth who should be educated first, and only then their elders. However, Socrates states clearly in *Apology* 23c that he never sought to teach the youth, but that they merely congregated about him to see their elders embarrassed by his questions. A careful examination of Plato's other dialogues, *Theaetetus* and *Lysis*, for example, confirms that Socrates continually attempts to turn the arguments to the adults, using youths as props to force their seniors to give answer. So, whether Socrates taught the youth or not, it is clearly Plato's representation that he did not. However, the whole question is more complicated than one would at first assume: *"At least, that would be the likely outcome to one beginning from such a beginning."*

The attitude of many prominent Athenians seems to have coincided with the opinions of Callicles, whom Plato uses in *Gorgias* as a disparager of late philosophical studies. His cavils are well worth reading in order to grasp Plato's answer:

> Well then, that is the truth, and you will come to know it once you have left behind philosophy and moved on to greater things. For philosophy is a graceful thing, Socrates, if someone is, in due measure, attached to it in that time of life; but if one spends time in it beyond what he ought, it is the ruin of men. For, though he be well grown, should he philosophize beyond his youth, he will necessarily be inexperienced in those things with which a man must familiarize himself if he would be beautiful, noble, and of good repute. For they are inexpert in the laws of their city and in the language that they must employ with people when making public and private contracts, as well as in human pleasures and wants. In sum, they are in all respects inexperienced with the characters of men. And, therefore, approaching some private or political matter, they become ridiculous, as at least, I think, statesmen are ridiculous when they come to your pastimes and arguments. (*Gorgias* 485c-e)

In essence, Callicles maintains that philosophy is of no consequence to the practical concerns of life, which culminate in the exercise of political power. Again, we find the question of public and private life raised explicitly. Philosophy teaches nothing about the law and it has nothing to say about human desires or the characters of men. Consequently, the philosopher must appear as a laughingstock whenever he approaches these matters. However, one needs merely to examine Plato's own works to see that the case is quite the opposite. They are filled with questions about human nature, moral duty, and the correct structure of the state.

In the *Republic*, Plato voices through Socrates an alternative view of education that puts philosophy at the pinnacle of life, making it to be a beatifying attainment that is genuinely beyond the capacity of adolescents:

> "Today," I said, "those who attach themselves to philosophy are mere youths, just out of childhood, who, in the interval between household rule and money-making, approach what I would say is the most difficult part of the subject, that which concerns arguments, and are then released from it. These are then made out to be the most philosophical of people. Later in life, they think it a great thing if, being summoned, they wish to be hearers of those who genuinely practice it, as they rather think it ought to be a hobby. Toward old age, they are, outside of a few, extinguished more completely than the sun of Heraclitus, inasmuch as they are, for their part, never rekindled." "But how ought it to be?" I replied. "Completely the opposite. While as yet boys and adolescents, they ought to lay their hands on an education

and philosophy suitable to youth and, caring very well for the bodies in which they are sprouting and growing to manhood, equip themselves for philosophy. Coming to the prime of life, when the soul begins to reach maturity, they should stretch out their exercises. Finally, when their bodily strength wanes, and they are past political and military duties, they should be allotted free range, doing nothing else but philosophize, except in passing. They would then live in a state of exceeding blessedness, and, having reached their end, come to know a conspicuous and merited reward for the life they have thus lived. (*Republic* 497e-498c)

Education should indeed begin with youths, but the material and method must be proportioned to their abilities. One should have no illusions about their power to argue philosophical questions. Rather, they should be made competent in foundational skills that will serve them later. Otherwise, their early exposure to higher studies will extinguish completely and permanently their desire for learning. It is for this reason that Socrates is guarded in his approval of attending to the education of youths: "*At least, that would be the likely outcome to one beginning from such a beginning.*"

One of the points made in Plato's *Phaedrus* is that understanding will only come through sowing the proper seeds in the student, which demands that these seeds consist not in written letters, but in the word that is conceived in the soul of the hearer:

> **Socrates:** For writing, Phaedrus, has in some degree this danger and is truly something like a scene-painting. For the offspring of the latter stand like living things, but, if you ask something, they are altogether and gravely silent. Written words are the same. You would think that they speak as though understanding something, but if you question them, wishing to learn something of their sayings, they always indicate only one and the same thing. And, once one writes, every word is bandied about, in like manner by those who have an ear to understand it and by those to whom it is not at all fitting. The word does not know to whom it ought or ought not to speak. And when being wronged or reviled unjustly, it always needs the assistance of its father, for it is powerless to either defend or assist itself.
>
> **Phaedrus:** You have said these things most correctly as well.
>
> **Socrates:** But what then? Do we see another word, the legitimate brother of this one, both in the manner it is begotten and in the better and more powerful way it grows?
>
> **Phaedrus:** What is this word, and how do you say that it is begotten?
>
> **Socrates:** That which is written with knowledge in the soul of the learner, having the power to defend itself and knowing to whom it is fitting to speak and to whom to be silent.
>
> **Phaedrus:** You speak of the living and ensouled word of the one who knows, of which the written word may justly be called the image. (*Phaedrus*, 275d-276a)

The distinction between the written word and the word of understanding answers to the distinction between body and soul, which becomes central to the very meaning of *Euthyphro*. The Socratic method of education is a meeting of two souls, one of which can judge the understanding of the other and fit its instruction to that understanding. It is not the meeting of a soul and the bodily word, a meeting that is liable to be misunderstood by the student, which can lead to parroting of words and a remarkable appearance of progress, but without genuine substance:

> **Socrates:** Altogether so. But just tell me this: A mindful husbandmen who is concerned for his seeds and wishes them to become fruitful, would he, plowing in earnest gardens of Adonis during the summer, rejoice to watch them become beautiful in eight days, or would he instead do these things, when he even does them, only for the sake of amusement and a holiday. Would he not instead, consulting the art of husbandry, earnestly sow into suitable soil, and be contented if that which he sowed reached maturity in the eighth month?
>
> **Phaedrus:** He would likely do things in the latter way, Socrates, when in earnest, and, as you say, in the former way when otherwise.
>
> **Socrates:** And should we assert that he who has knowledge of just and beautiful and good things possesses less mind concerning his seeds than does the husbandman.
>
> **Phaedrus:** Not at all.
>
> **Socrates:** Then, when in earnest, he will not write them in black ink, sowing through a reed with words powerless to defend themselves through argument, powerless to adequately teach the truth.
>
> **Phaedrus:** It is quite unlikely.
>
> **Socrates:** No, for he will sow gardens in letters, it would seem, only for the sake of amusement, and will write, whenever he does write, by making a treasury of reminders, both for himself when he comes to the Lethe of old age and for all who follow in his footsteps, and he will take pleasure in watching them put forth tender shoots. When others take part in amusements, drinking at banquets and other kindred things, that man will pass the time amusing himself with the things I describe, instead of these others. (*Phaedrus* 275d-276d)

Gardens of Adonis were a feature of the festival of Adonia,[3] which recalled the death of Adonis, one of Aphrodite's lovers. These gardens consisted of fennel seeds which sprouted in terra cotta, but then quickly withered and died. Plato has made this a figure of that sort of education which does not take root in the soul and subsequently perishes for lack of nourishment. The written word can only serve to remind one of what he already knows. So, he will write to help him recollect these truths in old age. Lethe was for the ancient Greeks one of the five rivers of the Underworld. Drinking from it caused forgetfulness.

Starting from the Hearth

Euthyphro: I would wish it so, Socrates, but I fear that the opposite may happen. For, in undertaking to wrong you, he seems to me to begin an artless work of evil against the city, starting from the hearth...

Meletus is acting artlessly because he acts without knowledge. His injustice works evil, "*starting from the hearth.*" By this one must not only understand "starting from the top" or "in its core" or some similar expression. The expression, "*starting from the hearth,*" though a common Greek expression, is used by Plato to invoke powerful associations.

Just as every household had a hearth (ἑστία) in which fire had to be maintained, so likewise the city-state. The common hearth (κοινή ἑστία) of the city-state was in the Prytaneum[4], a public building considered the symbolic center of the city, in which the prytanes (πρυτάνεις) conducted their business. The prytanes were fed at public expense in the Prytaneum. In Plato's *Apology*, Socrates taunts his accusers that as a punishment for his work he should receive such maintenance in the Prytaneum, which was an honor very rarely conferred. However, the reference contains a great deal more than this.

To appreciate the whole symbolism of the hearth, one must begin by examining Hestia (Ἑστία) the goddess named precisely for the hearth. *Euthyphro* is not the only dialogue in which Plato employs this expression. He uses the same in *Cratylus*: "But what now? Shall we begin, according to custom, from Hestia?" (*Cratylus* 401b) The playful etymologies found in *Cratylus* should not be taken seriously as genuine linguistic analyses of Greek names, but rather as a cipher by which we can read the other dialogues. *Cratylus* is rarely if ever recognized for this unique role. In this lexicon, "Hestia" means "essence," as Socrates explains to Hermogenes in the same dialogue:

> An example of such is that which we call οὐσία ("essence"), others call ἐσσία, and still others call ὡσία. First, then, in accordance with the second name, it is logical that the essence of things be called "Hestia" (Ἑστία); and furthermore, because we say of that which partakes of essence that "it is" (ἔστιν), in this respect it would also rightly be called "Hestia." For it seems that we also called οὐσία ("essence") ἐσσία in ancient times. Moreover, considering things according to the sacrifices, you would be led to conclude that those who established these names understood them in this same way. For whosoever has given the name ἐσσία to the essence (οὐσία) of all things, would likely sacrifice first to Hestia. (*Cratylus* 401c)

Plato introduces through Socrates the notion that the goddess Hestia, the traditional goddess of the hearth, is none other than essence. Essence, for Plato, is the primary object of knowledge:

34

> For the colorless, figureless, and intangible but really existing essence, the source of true knowledge, possesses this region and is to be seen only by the mind, the steersman of the soul. (*Phaedrus* 247c-d)

To work harm against the state by prosecuting Socrates then means not only to harm the state at its core, but to attack its very essence and divine model. In accord with tradition, Socrates tells us that Hestia does not leave her station: "For Hestia alone remains in the house of the gods." (*Phaedrus* 247a) For essence, precisely as essence, does not mingle with material bodies, but remains superior to them. Inferior realities may participate essences insofar as they share in the formal character of a particular essence, as a good man becomes good by participating in the Good, but they do not thereby become essences. An Idea's status as essence cannot itself be participated, for it is not an essence by virtue of its formal character, as will be seen as the dialogue progresses.

Yet Plato evokes even more by this expression, "*starting from the hearth.*" The mother of Socrates, Phaenarete, was a midwife, and Socrates therefore claimed for himself some share in the art:

> For this pertains to me as to midwives: I am childless with respect to wisdom. And that which many have reproached me with, namely, that I question others but that I myself make nothing of a reply about anything, because I possess no wisdom, that is indeed a truthful reproach. But the cause of it is this: the god compels me to serve as midwife but has prevented me from conceiving. I am then not at all someone wise, nor do I have some such discovery, a child begotten of my own soul. But those associating with me, though at first some appear quite devoid of learning, yet all those applying themselves, whomever the god allows, share in the great and wonderful progress, as it appears both to them and to others. And it is manifest that they learn nothing whatsoever from me, but that they have discovered and brought forth many beautiful things of themselves. But the god and I are the cause of the delivery. (*Theaetetus* 150c-d)

Socrates rarely puts forth his own notions explicitly in the dialogues, except as proposals designed to probe the opinions of his interlocutors. Like a midwife (*maia*, μαῖα), Socrates claims no parentage of any notion; he instead aids in its delivery. His method of education, literally an educing of truths from the questioned soul, is consequently called the Socratic Maieutic. This conversational form of questioning and answering is also what Plato calls dialectic (διάλεξις). Through dialectic one's opinions are run round about as one circles in upon an understanding of genuine essences. It is for this reason that Plato, through the character of Socrates, describes the process in terms of the traditional Greek practice called Amphidromy (ἀμφιδρόμια). After the birth of a child, the midwife would ceremonially carry the newborn about the hearth to be presented to the household gods and the family members. The father would thereafter, in the ancient tradition, decide whether the child was worthy to be reared or exposed. Socrates explains the educational process to Theaetetus in the dialogue bearing the latter's name:

Well, it would seem we have at long length only just begotten this, whatever it chances to be. And after the delivery, in accordance with the festival of the carrying about the hearth, the offspring must be run around in the circle of our argument, being examined, lest it escape our notice, whether it may be unworthy of nourishment, a mere wind-egg and imposture. (*Theaetetus* 160e-161a)

This "festival of carrying about the hearth," the Amphidromy, thus becomes the very image of the dialectical process of assessing one's opinions, and the question of whether to nourish the offspring is decided by its conformity to the essence being investigated. From this is derived a final significance of "*starting from the hearth*": By wronging Socrates, Meletus harms the educational capacity of the state.

A Maker of Gods

Euthyphro: ... *But tell me, what does he say you do to corrupt the young?*
Socrates: *Outlandish things, wondrous man, at least to hear it in this way. For he says that I am a maker of gods, and, for making fresh gods and not recognizing the ancient ones, he has brought an indictment against me on behalf of the latter, or so he says.*

Euthyphro presses Socrates as to the charges on which he has been indicted. The charges are more precisely outlined by Socrates in Plato's *Apology*: "Socrates is an evildoer and a meddler, seeking out things both under the earth and in the heavens, and making the weaker argument the stronger and teaching others these same things." (*Apology* 19b-c) As one "seeking out things both under the earth and in the heavens," Socrates is being lumped together with the natural philosophers, who had called into question the tenets and tales of the ancient religion. In *Phaedrus* Plato makes a telling comparison between the attitudes of Socrates and the natural philosophers. The context is the story of Boreas and Pharmacea. Greek religious tradition held that Boreas, the god of the North Wind, had abducted the girl, Oreithyia, as she played with Pharmacea, the nymph of the river Ilissus. Socrates tells Phaedrus that he thinks the materialistic explanations are of little worth:

If I disbelieved, as do the wise men, I would not appear outlandish. Then, being made wise, I would say that a blast of Boreas, the North Wind, threw her from the neighboring rocks while she was playing with Pharmacea and, having died in this way, she was carried away by Boreas. But I think, Phaedrus, that such explanations, being otherwise rather elegant, are the mark of a quite wearisome and not altogether fortunate man. (*Phaedrus* 229 c-d)

Plato uses the adjective, ἄτοπος, which has been translated "outlandish" in keeping with both contexts. It has a more literal meaning of "without place." It is no accident that the term appears in both dialogues when Socrates speaks of his attitude toward the gods. The materialists maintained that all beings are bodies and therefore exist in a place. Plato's belief in the spiritual and incorporeal nature of divinity necessarily locates them outside of place, if one may even speak coherently of their location. Place is a principle of multitude; Ideas are both individual and unique, not multiplied in different matter or receptables. For Plato, the proper attitude is not to disbelieve these stories by supplying a material explanation that subverts their meaning, but to see them as a mythical expression of a higher truth. This latter treatment of the gods is pursued consistently in *Euthyphro* and Plato's other dialogues and is likely the manner in which Socrates himself spoke about them. So, there is perhaps some truth in this claim of Meletus that Socrates does not believe in the traditional gods. Indeed, a rational person could hardly accept these stories at face-value, and this left the philosophers quite vulnerable to both personal and political attacks from their enemies.

There is yet more. The claim that Socrates is creating new gods is indeed outlandish, "*at least to hear it in this way.*" This qualification so thoroughly undermines the rejection of the claim that one must ask: In what way then is Socrates genuinely making gods? The answer is that Plato sometimes uses "god" to refer not to the divine ideas themselves, but to the philosophers divinized by their intellection of the ideas:

> **Theaetetus:** Though the man does not at all seem to me to be a god, he seems to be divine, for I address all philosophers as such.
>
> **Socrates:** And beautifully so, my friend. And yet, as one might say, it may chance that it is not much easier to distinguish this class than that of the gods. (*Sophist* 216b-c)

Philosophers are more properly called "divine." However, were one to speak of philosophers as gods, there would be a good deal of truth in it. Socrates is making new gods by teaching, and the old gods, particularly the sophists and their students, are none too pleased about it.

Socrates and His Spirit (Δαίμων)

Euthyphro: I am beginning to understand, Socrates. It is no doubt because you say that a spirit visits you from time to time. He has therefore brought this indictment against you for making innovations about divine matters, and he comes into the court slandering, knowing that such things are easily received by the multitude. Why, they even ridicule me as a madman whenever I say something in the assembly concerning divine matters, foretelling to them things that will be. And yet not one of the things I have foretold is untrue. All the same, they are jealous of all people such as ourselves. Do not allow your understanding to be occupied with them, but rather come to close quarters with them.

Euthyphro's recollection of Socrates' "spirit" or "daimon" (δαίμων) serves to further specify Plato's intended meaning. This matter of the δαίμων was most famously taken up by Heraclitus when he stated: Ἔθος ἀνθρώπῳ δαίμων. Ἔθος can be translated as "habit" or "character" and ἀνθρώπῳ means "for a man" or "belonging to a man." Translating δαίμων is problematic. It can mean "guardian spirit" or, more simply, "fate" or "destiny." One straightforward rendering of the saying of Heraclitus is "A man's character is his destiny." However, the saying is necessarily flexible and nuanced. Plato treats the question in *Cratylus*:

Socrates: Hermogenes, what does the name "spirits" (δαίμονες) truly mean? See if you think there is something to what I will say.

Hermogenes: Just say it.

Socrates: Don't you know who Hesiod says the spirits are?

Hermogenes: No. I don't.

Socrates: Nor that a golden race was the first race of men to be born?

Hermogenes: That, at least, I do know.

Socrates: Well, he says this of it:

"But since Fate has buried this race,

They are called pure spirits under the earth,

Good, warding off evils, sentinels of mortal men."

Hermogenes: What then?

Socrates: Well, I think he means that the golden race was not brought forth of gold but was good and beautiful. And that he says that we are fashioned of iron is for me a sure sign.

Hermogenes: What you say is true.

Socrates: Would you suppose, therefore, that if anyone today is likewise good, he is also of that golden race?

Hermogenes: Very likely.

38

Socrates: But are the good anything other than those with understanding?

Hermogenes: None other than those with understanding.

Socrates: Then it seems to me that he says this especially of the spirits, calling them "spirits" (δαίμονες) because they were understanding and knowing (δαήμ ονες); and in our ancient dialect the names come together. Both Hesiod and many other poets speak beautifully, as many as say that whenever some good man has finished his life, he receives a great portion and honor, and becomes a spirit (δαίμων) in accordance with that which is named from "understanding" (φρονήσεως). For this reason, I assert that every man, whether living or dead, if he be good, is spiritual and is rightly called a spirit (δαίμων). (*Cratylus* 397e-398c)

Gold in Plato is synonymous with the Good. In the *Symposium*, Pausanias describes the method of testing for potential relationships in terms of the touchstone, a black stone which, when rubbed against a metal, shows by the streak whether it be genuine or false gold:

"Now our good and beautiful custom is to rub these persons with the touchstone, which tells us which to favor and which to shun. Through this process then it prescribes pursuing some, and fleeing from the others." (*Symposium* 184a)

Whereas the spirit (δαίμων) of Heraclitus could be either good or evil, depending upon the character of the man, Plato appears to have reserved the term for the good alone. The δαίμων of a man is his spiritual participation in the Good, made possible by his understanding, so Plato logically extends the term to the living as well, although in the proper sense of the word a good man "becomes a spirit (δαίμων)" only at death. Socrates receives only warnings that forbid him to perform certain actions, but never commands to perform others. In this respect, one could loosely translate the δαίμων of Socrates as "conscience," keeping in mind that the good who have died have a more perfect relation to the Good. However, this is too limited a notion.

According to the teaching of Diotima related by Socrates in the *Symposium*, the spirits lie midway between the mortal and the immortal. They are manifold, and include Desire:

"But you have agreed that Desire, for a lack of good and beautiful things, desires these same things that it lacks."

"I have."

"How then would one who has no portion of beautiful and good things be a god?"

"In no way, it seems."

"Then you see," she said, "you do not consider Desire a god."

"What then would Desire be?" I asked. "A mortal?"

"That least of all."

"But what?"

"As I said previously, something between the mortal and immortal."

"What then, Diotima?"

"A great spirit, Socrates: for every spiritual thing is between the divine and the mortal."

"What power does it have?" I asked.

"That of interpreting and transmitting what is of men to the gods, and what is of the gods to men: petitions and sacrifices from men, commandments and recompense from the gods. Being in the middle, it completes both, so that each is perfectly bound to the other. Through it is dispensed all prophecy, all of the priestly arts concerning sacrifice, ritual and incantation, and all soothsaying and magic. God does not mingle with man, but all communion and conversation between men and gods is through the spiritual, whether one is asleep or has awakened. He who is wise in these matters is the spiritual man, but he who is wise in other matters, in mechanical arts and handicraft, is an artisan. These spirits are multitudinous and of every kind, and Desire is one of them. (*Symposium* 202d-203a)

Socrates is one who communes with the divine, that is to say with the Ideas. His spirit (δαίμων) mediates between these levels of being. In this respect, the mention of the spirit of Socrates anticipates the later claim that holiness conveys a knowledge of prayer and sacrifice.

One may be tempted to identify Plato's "spirit" with divine grace as it is understood in Catholic Christianity. This temptation exists because Plato never adequately demarcated the natural and supernatural. There would seem to be a participation in the divine Ideas by man. However, Plato posits human understanding as adequate to the divine Ideas. The participation is through a purely natural knowledge of essences. It is chiefly in his Pelagian notion of man and his relation to divinity that Plato's "spiritual" deviates from the Christian doctrine of grace, which is a divine gift producing and grounded in an act of faith, rather than the natural effect of intellectual vision. It is for this reason that Christian theologians who followed a Platonic line of thinking were forced to introduce the notion of divine illumination, which posits God as an immediate cause and initiator of knowledge. This effectively nullified the Pelagian interpretation.

The Teaching of Wisdom

Socrates: *But, Euthyphro, my friend, perhaps their ridicule is of no matter. For it is of no violent concern to the Athenians if they consider someone to be clever, at least it seems to me, provided he is not fit to teach his wisdom. But whenever they think he makes others to be such a sort as well, they become angry, either from envy, as you say, or on account of something else.*

The teachability of wisdom and virtue is a prominent theme in Plato's dialogues. The capacity to teach depends upon the possession of knowledge, something that Socrates has shown again and again to be lacking in precisely those who profess to have it. This breeds in these humiliated men an envy. Moreover, they feel threatened in their power by any questioning that exposes their limitations. Even the better sort of ruler governs not from genuine knowledge, but from correct opinion, obtained from whatever source:

> **Socrates:** Then it is not by any wisdom, or because they were wise, that men of this sort led their cities, both Themistocles and those men of whom Anytus here spoke just now. Wherefore, they cannot make others of the same sort as themselves because it is not knowledge that makes them of such a sort.
>
> **Meno:** It would seem to be as you say, Socrates.
>
> **Socrates:** Therefore, if not by knowledge, then it happens by good opinion. Statesmen use this to set their cities straight, differing not at all in understanding from those chanting oracles or delivering prophecies. For the latter also speak many truths but know nothing of what they say. (*Meno*, 99b-c)

Thus, it happens that men of natural endowment and high achievement, men such as Themistocles, failed to educate their own sons in their supposed wisdom, for it was not really wisdom by which they governed, but sound opinion. The same can be said of the poets, an accusation he repeats in the *Apology*:

> Then also concerning the poets, I came to know in a little time this: that not by wisdom do they make the things they make, but by a certain nature and by being inspired, just like divine prophets and those who chant oracles; for these also speak many beautiful things but have understood nothing of the things they say. (*Apology* 22b-c)

Neither the political men nor the poets have turned their intellectual vision toward the Ideas that govern the world around them. Socrates, on the other hand, like Teiresias, the blind prophet in *Oedipus the King*, has acquired that vision:

> Teiresias, you are versed in everything,
> things teachable and things not to be spoken,
> things of the heaven and earth-creeping things.
> You have no eyes but in your mind you know
> with what a plague our city is afflicted.
> (*Oedipus the King*, 300-303)

He is consequently able to transmit his knowledge to others, which for Plato means to lead their intellectual gaze to the divine Ideas, the patterns in which the material world participates. Note that "things of the heaven and earth-creeping things" corresponds approximately to the accusation made against Socrates: "seeking out things both under the earth and in the heavens."

Euthyphro: *Well, I have no great wish to test exactly how they regard me in this.*

Socrates observes that the reason that Euthyphro has not aroused the anger of the city is that he is unwilling to teach. He makes himself "scarce," implying not only that Euthyphro does not make himself available, but that he views knowledge, supposing that he even has it, as a commodity. On the other hand, Socrates through his maieutic art not only teaches without a fee, but would pay his students to learn. He is indeed a gift to the city, giving himself without demand of return or recompense:

> "But that I happen to be a sort of gift of the god to the city, you may observe well from this: It does not belong to human nature that I have neglected all of my things and for so many years have borne the neglect of my domestic affairs, but am rather always minding your own, approaching each of you as would a father or an elder brother, urging you to bestow care upon virtue. And if I benefited in any way from these things or made a profit from recommending such things, it might have some rationale. But now you see for yourselves that my accusers, though they accuse me thus so shamefully of all other things, have not behaved so impudently as to have furnished a witness that I ever pressed anyone for pay, or even asked. For I think that I have furnished a sufficient witness that I speak truly: my poverty." (*Apology* 31a-c)

Socrates is taking aim at those sophists, men who profess themselves wise, who travel from city to city enriching themselves by their teaching. He says ironically at his trial:

> "Now this also seems to me to be a beautiful thing if someone were of such a sort as to instruct people—as Gorgias of Leontini, Prodicus of Ceos, and Hippias of Elis are. For, gentlemen, each of these men is of such a sort that, going into each of the cities, they persuade the young men, for whom it is permitted as a gift of the cities themselves to associate with whomever they wish, to leave behind their associations with those men and associate with themselves instead, pay them money, and be grateful moreover." (*Apology* 19e-20a)

Yet these salesmen, these purveyors of wisdom, so called, really have no understanding of the benefit or harm that comes to those who are nourished upon it:

> "Then, Hippocrates, is the sophist perchance a merchant or retailer of the wares by which the soul is nourished?"
>
> "With what is the soul nourished, Socrates?"
>
> "Presumably with learning," I replied. "And let not the sophist deceive us, commending his wares as the merchant and retailer do concerning the nourishment of the body. For the latter are ignorant of whether the wares they sell are injurious or useful to the body, since they commend all the things they sell, and so do those buying from them, unless someone chances to be a trainer or doctor." (*Protagoras* 313c-313d)

So, in the end, what are these sophists? The Stranger in the *Sophist* at length provides a humorous definition:

> The sophist, it appears, is nothing other than the commercial class of the captious, quarrelsome, disputatious, pugnacious, contentious, acquisitive art, as our argument has now once again disclosed. (*Sophist* 226a)

And here Plato, no doubt, agrees with the words placed into the mouth of Anytus, an accuser of Socrates who ultimately could not discern the difference between Socrates and the sophists:

> Heracles, Socrates, keep a sacred silence! May such madness never seize anyone of my household or among my friends, whether citizen or foreigner, that he should be outraged by those invaders. For these men are clearly a disgrace and ruin to those associating with them. (*Meno* 91c)

It is no accident that Socrates time and again at his trial addresses the court as "men of Athens," as if to emphasize the foreign origin of these merchants of false wisdom who have invaded Athens and captured the youth.

... So, if, as I was just saying, they were to ridicule me, as you say of yourself, it would not be unpleasant to pass the time playing like children and laughing in the court. But if they are in haste, how this will turn out is unclear, except to you prophets.

The subtlety of the connections between dialogues can be judged by this reply of Socrates. Here he makes an oblique reference to a cipher established in *Gorgias,* in another portion of that diatribe of Callicles against those who continue the study of philosophy late into life:

> It is a beautiful thing to partake of philosophy for the sake of the education of youth, and it is not shameful for a youth to love philosophy, but when an elderly man still philosophizes, Socrates, the whole affair becomes ridiculous. I, for my own part, feel something very much like this toward those who philosophize, just as toward those who lisp or play children's games. For whenever I see a small child lisping and playing, I delight in it, and it appears free-spirited and seemly to that age, whereas, when I hear a little child conversing clearly, I feel the matter keenly. It grieves my ears and seems to me something befitting a slave. But when I hear a man lisping or see him playing children's games, it appears ridiculous and unmanly, worthy of a flogging. I feel this same thing also with regard to those who philosophize. For, seeing philosophy in a youth, I admire it, and it seems proper to me, and I consider this person to be free-spirited, whereas the one who does not philosophize I consider illiberal and incapable of expecting of himself any beautiful or well-begotten action. But when I see an elderly man still philosophizing, refusing to give it up, it seems to me, Socrates, that this is the man who needs a flogging. For, as I said just now, this man, though he be well developed, must become unmanly by fleeing from the center and marketplace of the city, in which, said the poet, "men become illustrious." He must live out the remainder

of his life sunk down, whispering with three or four youths, and never utter a liberal or great or vigorous word. (*Gorgias* 485a-d)

In typical Platonic fashion, the repeated references to playing children's games establishes a metaphor for the act of philosophizing. We may consequently understand Socrates to be saying that if they were "*to pass the time playing like children and laughing in court,*" that is, if the proceedings of the court were open to the dialectical method that Socrates practices, and if the court were sufficiently patient to wait for a satisfactory conclusion, it would be an altogether pleasant affair. On the other hand, if he were not allowed to state his case philosophically in the customary manner but were instead pressed for incomplete answers to poorly constructed questions, the outcome would be in serious jeopardy.

Euthyphro: *Well, Socrates, perhaps the matter will come to nothing, and you will carry the case in accordance with your own mind, as I think that I shall also carry my own.*

Recall Euthyphro's claim, "*And yet not one of the things I have foretold is untrue.*" Here Euthyphro reveals that he is indeed a very poor prophet, for Socrates will not only fail to acquit himself, but will even be put to death as a punishment.

Bipeds, Feathered and Featherless

Socrates: *And what is your suit, Euthyphro? Are you fleeing (defending) or pursuing (prosecuting)?*

Euthyphro: *I am pursuing.*

The terms used specifically for prosecuting and defending, διώκεις and φεύγεις, also have the more general meaning of "pursuing" and "fleeing." Once again, however, Plato's *Cratylus,* dealing explicitly with the correctness of names, permits Plato to create a fanciful vocabulary for expressing his philosophy. By using this resource, one can discover a deeper meaning in the words of Socrates and Euthyphro:

"Opinion" (δόξα) is named either from pursuit (δίωξις), that which the soul is made to undertake as it pursues the knowledge of things, or from the "shooting" (βολή) of the bow (τόξον); it would rather seem to be the latter. At any rate, "sentiment" (οἴησις) harmonizes with that, for it resembles the "motion" (οἶσις) of the soul toward all things such as they are, as also "intention" (βουλή) resembles "shooting" (βολή) and "to wish" (βούλεσθαι) and "to plan" (βουλεύεσθαι) signify launching at. All these things seem to follow "opinion" (δόξα) and copy after "shooting" (βολή), just as ill-advisedness (ἀβουλία) seems to be a mischance or miscarriage, as of someone not shooting or hitting that which he shot at, wished, planned, or launched at. (*Cratylus* 420b-c)

Euthyphro is pursuing; he is in a state of opinion (δόξα) as he pursues knowledge. He does not have knowledge itself, because his soul is turned not to the Ideas, but to mutable bodies. Another image that appears occasionally in the dialogue is that of shooting a bow. Euthyphro will attempt time and again to string the bow and strike the target, but he is found to continually "miss the mark" (ἐξαμαρτάνειν), falling into error (ἁμαρτία). This difference between opinion and knowledge is brought out in *Gorgias*:

> **Socrates:** Then does it seem to you that to have learned and to have believed or, alternatively, learning and belief, are the same thing, or something different?
>
> **Gorgias:** I myself would say that they are different, Socrates.
>
> **Socrates:** And you think beautifully. You may come to know it from this: For should someone ask you, "Gorgias, is there a false belief and a true belief?" You would, I think, affirm it.
>
> **Gorgias:** Yes.
>
> **Socrates:** But then is there a false knowledge and a true knowledge?
>
> **Gorgias:** By no means.
>
> **Socrates:** Then it is again clear that they are not the same.
>
> **Gorgias:** You speak the truth. (*Gorgias* 454d)

Euthyphro, like the poets and politicians, speaks from opinion, rather than from knowledge. Inasmuch as he is correct in his assertions, he has merely true opinion or belief.

Socrates: Whom?

Euthyphro: Someone I would seem mad to pursue.

Socrates: But why? Are you pursuing someone on the wing?

Euthyphro: He lacks much to fly, since he happens to be exceedingly old.

Socrates: Who is he?

Euthyphro: My father.

Socrates: Your own father, best of men?

Euthyphro: Most certainly.

This is one of several references to Sophocles' masterpiece, *Oedipus the King*. Socrates and Euthyphro stand in the Portico of the King. Plato would have us recall the exchange between Oedipus and the priest. Suppliants have come to beg the gods for an end to the plague that has come upon the city of Thebes. Oedipus, making himself out to be a god, assures the priest that he will take pity upon them:

Oedipus: Children, young sons and daughters of old Cadmus,
why do you sit here with your suppliant crowns?
the town is heavy with a mingled burden
of sounds and smells, of groans and hymns and incense;
I did not think it fit that I should hear
of this from messengers but came myself,—
I Oedipus whom all men call the Great.
[*He returns to the* PRIEST.]
You're old and they are young; come speak for them.
What do you fear or want, that you sit here
suppliant? Indeed I'm willing to give all
that you need; I would be very hard
should I not pity suppliants like these.
(*Oedipus the King,* 1-13)

It is the immediate response of the priest of Zeus to which Plato has alluded, thereby identifying Euthyphro with Oedipus, and Socrates, one of those "heavy with age," not only with the priest of Zeus, but with the fathers of Euthyphro and Oedipus:

Priest: O ruler of my country, Oedipus,
you see our company around the altar;
you see our ages; some of us, like these,
who cannot yet fly far, and some of us
heavy with age; these children are the chosen
among the young, and I the priest of Zeus.
(*Oedipus the King,* 14-19)

Oedipus is guilty of hubris toward the gods, daring to usurp their power, authority, and praise. He is, in a single word, impious. The priest later corrects Oedipus for the latter's grave misapprehension about his own divinity:

Priest: We have not come as suppliants to this altar
because we thought of you as a god,
but rather judging you the first of men
in all the chances of this life and when
we mortals have to do with more than man.
(*Oedipus the King,* 31-34)

Euthyphro has thus been identified with Oedipus, who murdered his father and married his mother, becoming a curse and a source of religious pollution to his native Thebes. Socrates, on the other hand, takes on the role here of "the priest of Zeus."

Socrates' reference to being "on the wing" has, however, a much deeper meaning. He is asking whether the man that Euthyphro pursues has flown above the corporeal world and entered the spiritual realm of the Ideas. The nature of man, to follow *Cratylus,* is to look up at the world above:

This name, "man" (ἄνθρωπος), points out that the other animals neither examine, nor reckon, nor look up at (ἀναθρεῖ) any of the things you see, but man, as soon as he has seen, that is ὄπωπε, both looks up (ἀναθρεῖ) and reckons that which he has seen (ὄπωπεν). Hence, of all the animals only man, looking up at (ἀναθρῶν) the things he has seen (ὄπωπε), is rightly named "man" (ἄνθρωπος). (*Cratylus* 399c)

However, unless one has entered deeply into philosophy, he remains a featherless biped:

For a man must comprehend under an idea the things that are spoken, raising by rational argument a multitude of sensations into a unified ensemble; and this is indeed the recollection of those things that our soul once beheld when it traveled with God, when, looking beyond the things that we now say exist, it raised its sight toward real being. Therefore, it is with justice that the philosopher's understanding is alone winged. For he is always, in keeping with his power, in communion through memory with those very things by which a god is divine. Now the man who uses those reminders rightly is always performing the perfect rites and he alone becomes perfect. However, because he stands apart from human pursuits and turns his mind toward the divine, he is treated badly by the common people, who fail to notice that he is divinely inspired. (*Phaedrus* 249b-d)

Note that recollection is "of those things that our soul once beheld when it traveled with God, when, looking beyond the things that we now say exist, it raised its sight toward real being." This traveling with God brings the reader back to the "*lack of learnedness*" (ἀμαθία) of Socrates and its derivation of the term from "the progression of he who goes together with God." The process of growing wings begins when an individual open to the truth encounters a man like Socrates, who is intellectually and spiritually beautiful, even if his physical appearance is repugnant. This encounter produces in him one of the spirits, philosophical Eros (ἔρως), a desire to beget upon the beautiful, as Diotima explained to Socrates:

"For Desire is not a desire for the beautiful, as you seem to think, Socrates."
"But for what then?"
"For begetting and giving birth upon the beautiful."
(*Symposium* 206e)

Eros (ἔρως), which may be translated as "love," physical or spiritual, has been translated as "desire," in keeping with Plato's affirmation through Diotima in the *Symposium* that there is a lack or privation in it. This keeps the notions of ἔρως (love as desire) and φιλία (love as friendship) sufficiently distinct. On account of this desire the individual begins to sprout feathers:

Receiving the effluence of beauty through the eyes, he is warmed, and the shoots of the feathers are moistened and, being warmed where the growth of the feather is, those parts about the germinating feathers which were once very hard and constricted, preventing the feathers from sprouting, begin to soften. And as nourishment streams upon them, the feathers swell and begin to sprout from the root, thence to the stem and to the whole form of the soul. For it was once completely feathered. (*Phaedrus* 251b)

In its prior existence, before it sank into the corporeal and became enamored of bodies, the soul was completely feathered. Feathered wings give the power of upward flight into the divine regions of intellect. They are fed only by "the beautiful, the wise, the good, and all things of such a sort," but destroyed by their opposites:

> The natural power of the wing is to draw a weight upward, lifting it on high to where the race of gods dwells. It especially, more than the other things that pertain to the body, partakes of the divine. But the divine itself is the beautiful, the wise, the good, and all things of such a sort. By these especially the wings of the soul are nourished and increased, but by the shameful, the evil, and the other opposites, they waste away and are utterly destroyed. (*Phaedrus* 246d-e)

"Guileless and buoyant" men, who may have previously attended to the cosmos through their senses, are transformed into birds capable of flying into the regions of pure mind:

> And the race of birds, growing feathers in place of hair, are thus transformed out of guileless and buoyant men, including those skilled in the knowledge of the heavens, who in their simple-mindedness suppose that demonstrations of these matters through the sense of sight are the most certain. (*Timaeus* 91d-91e)

The soul then soars by its recovered wings into the highest realities, intuiting directly and without the aid of the senses the intelligible realities that stand above the corporeal world:

> If someone should come to the very summit of the air or becoming winged should fly up and raise his head above to make a survey, just as fish lifting their heads hither out of the sea observe things here, so also would he see everything there; and if his nature were sufficient to withstand the contemplation of those things, he would recognize them as the true heaven, and the true light, and the true earth. (*Phaedo* 109e-110a)

These are the regions of genuine being, lacking extension and all bodily attributes, but consisting in unchanging essences, the Ideas in which bodies merely participate. That Plato taught such things is beyond doubt, but it appears that outside of his circle of students, the meaning of such metaphors was not properly apprehended. Diogenes Laertius tells of the encounter between Plato and Diogenes the Cynic:

> Plato being esteemed for having made the definition, "Man is a featherless bipedal animal," [Diogenes] carried into the school a plucked fowl and said, "This is Plato's man!" Whence there was added to the definition "having flat nails." (*Lives of the Eminent Philosophers* VI.40)

Plato clearly did not intend that the meaning of his doctrines should be apprehended by just anyone who happened to hear him speak, but only by those he deemed worthy of instruction.

Familial Duty

Socrates: But what is the charge, and what does the suit concern?

Euthyphro: Murder, Socrates.

Socrates: Heracles! I suppose, Euthyphro, that the multitude does not know where the right lies. For I do not think it the part of just anyone to do it rightly, but only of the one driving wisdom somewhere very far.

Euthyphro: By Zeus, very far indeed, Socrates.

Socrates: But was the person killed by your father one of your relatives? But of course! For surely you would not charge him with murder for the sake of a stranger.

Because the Idea is one, whereas the bodily instances are multitudinous, one cannot come to know the truth of things by turning to the many, whether they be many instances or many opinions. Plato plays humorously with the expression "*one driving wisdom somewhere very far.*" It is an ambivalent expression: Is Socrates praising Euthyphro for the extent he has pursued wisdom, or criticizing him for having driven wisdom far away? This is not the only instance of the expression in Plato. After another Socratic bout of deriving names from absurd origins, Hermogenes addresses Socrates:

> **Hermogenes:** Truly, Socrates, you have bestowed a great deal.
>
> **Socrates:** Yes, for I appear already to be driving wisdom very far. (*Cratylus* 410e)

The image of driving oxen, which is the oxherd's art, is used in contexts in which Plato is treating of rhetoric. Leaving aside the question of whether Euthyphro has acted properly or not, the correct use of rhetoric is not to defend injustice in the courts, but to convince the unjust, whether oneself or another, to submit willingly to a just punishment. In this way alone can one purify oneself or lead another to do the same:

> **Socrates:** But if either he, or someone else over whom he troubles himself, has committed an injustice, he must go willingly where he will most speedily pay the penalty, to the side of the judge, just as to a doctor, hastening that the disease of injustice will not become chronic and form an incurable abscess of the soul. What else shall we say, Polus, if our earlier conclusions stand fast? Is it not necessary that these things harmonize with the former thus and in no other way?
>
> **Polus:** Indeed, Socrates, for what else should we say?
>
> **Socrates:** Then rhetoric, Polus, is of no use to us for making a defense on behalf of injustice, whether it is oneself, one's parents, comrades, children, or fatherland that has acted unjustly, unless, that is, we were to take up the opposite, that one ought first and foremost to accuse himself, and then his household and others who, yet being friends, happen to

act unjustly, not hiding away the wrongdoing, but making it manifest in order that he may pay the penalty and become healthy, compelling both himself and others not to shrink away, but to submit manfully with shut eyes to the surgeon's cutting and burning, pursuing the noble and the beautiful without calculation of the pain: When he has acted unjustly, if deserving of a flogging to submit to blows, if deserving of bonds to be bound, if deserving of a penalty to pay it, if deserving of exile to be banished, or if deserving death to be executed. He himself will be the first accuser, both of himself and the other members of his household and will use his rhetoric that he may make manifest their wrongdoing and that they may be released from the greatest evil, namely, injustice itself. Should we speak thus or not, Polus? (*Gorgias* 480a-d)

Implicit in this argument is that punishment is indeed a good, insofar as it deters the soul from evil and leads it back to the Good.

Euthyphro: It is ridiculous, Socrates, that you think it differs whether the man who was killed was a stranger or belonged to the household, whereas this alone must be safeguarded, whether the slayer slew in justice and if in justice, to allow it, but if not, to begin proceedings, even if the murderer is of a common hearth with you and shares a common table...

The "*common hearth*" refers to the household, whether of the family, of the state, or of the philosophers. The Athenian stranger in Plato's *Laws* is explicit about duties toward parents:

For these it is laid down that those in debt repay the first and greatest of debts, the most ancient of obligations, that he should acknowledge that everything that he has acquired and possesses belongs to those who begot and reared him, to the end of serving them to the best of his ability with these very things, beginning with his property, second with his body, and third with his soul, thus paying back the loans of care and the pangs of longstanding toil invested in their young and making recompense to them when they are wanting in old age. And throughout his whole life he must show restraint toward his parents, especially as regards reverence in speech, because for light and winged words there is a most heavy penalty, for, watching over such things in all situations, there has been stationed Nemesis, messenger of Justice. He must therefore yield to them when they are angry and appease them when they express their anger in either words or deeds, confessing that it is most reasonable for a father to be especially angry when he believes that he has been wronged by a son. (*Laws* 717b-d)

Clearly, Euthyphro is obliged out of respect for his father to forgive him, restraining his own passions, whether or not these feelings are justified. The debt to parents cannot be erased, for we have nothing of our own with which to repay them. A similar and even more pertinent criticism is found in *Protagoras*, when Socrates interprets the poem of Simonides:

For he considered that the good and beautiful man many times compels himself to befriend and commend someone, as when it happens that a man has a most distempered mother or father or country or anything of such a sort. But the wicked, whenever some such thing befalls them, as if well pleased, both display their censures and denounce the wickedness of their parents or country, in order that people may not charge them of neglect or reproach them for being negligent, with the result that they censure their parents all the more and add voluntary to inevitable enmities. But the good throw a cloak over the matter and compel themselves to approve, and if they are somehow angered by their parents or country doing wrong to them, they mollify and reconcile themselves, compelling themselves to love and commend their own. (*Protagoras* 345e-346b)

Here, the parallel between the family and the state is explicit. Whether the supposed offender is a parent or one's very country, a man must overlook the fault and continue to "love and praise." If indeed Socrates is something of a father in relation to a young man such as Meletus, we may infer that Meletus, whatever slight he may have received from Socrates, is completely unjustified in indicting him for impiety. Were Meletus a good and just man, he would have reconciled himself to Socrates. Instead, like Oedipus, he unwittingly curses himself:

Oedipus: Upon the murderer I invoke this curse—
whether he is one man and all unknown,
or one of many—may he wear out his life
in misery to miserable doom!
If with my knowledge he lives at my hearth
I pray that I myself may feel my curse.
(*Oedipus the King*, 246-251)

Like Oedipus, Euthyphro, together with Meletus, whom he represents, does not know who his father is.

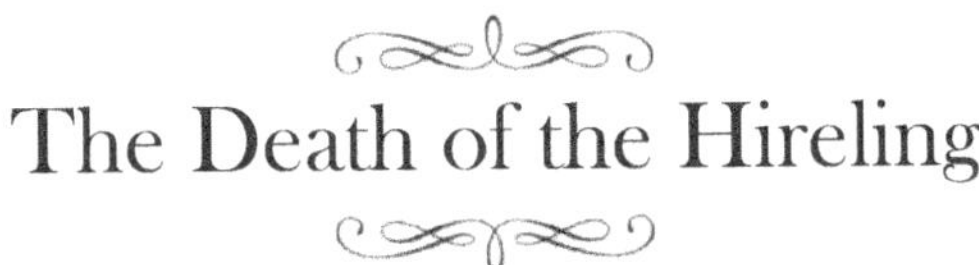

The Death of the Hireling

... For an equal pollution takes place if you knowingly associate with such a man, and do not purify both yourself and him by bringing suit.

  Euthyphro's concept of purity is a merely legal one that does not touch upon the character of the man himself. It is to be achieved through the courts by a legal proceeding against those who have been polluted by their actions. According to tradition, the punishment Meletus meted out to Socrates ultimately redounded to his own head, just as it did to Oedipus:

Creon: I will tell you, then,
what I heard from the god.
King Phoebus in plain words commanded us

> to drive out a pollution from our land;
> drive it out, said the god, not cherish it,
> till it's past cure.

Oedipus: What is the rite
of purification? How shall it be done?

Creon: By banishing a man, or expiation
of blood by blood, since it is murder guilt
which holds our city in this destroying storm.
(*Oedipus the King*, 95-101)

Contrast Euthyphro's legalistic notion of purity with Plato's, as voiced in *Phaedo* through Socrates:

> And does not purification consist in that which was said long ago in the discussion: in separating as much as possible the soul from the body and in forming the habit of collecting and assembling itself from every part of the body, and dwelling, to the extent of its power, both in the present and hereafter, alone and in accord with itself, freed from the body just as if from bonds? (*Phaedo* 67c-d)

And how is this to be achieved? It can only be through the acquisition of understanding, a turning of the soul away from the senses toward the unchanging Ideas. Purification does not consist in a merely exterior ritual or exchange, but in an interior process, which Socrates claims to be the true nature of the secret Eleusinian rites:

> To exchange pleasure for pleasure, pain for pain, and fear for fear, the greater for the less, as if coins, may not be the right way to purchase virtue. But this rather is the only right coin: understanding, for which all of those things must be exchanged and by which and with which all them must be bought and sold. Courage, self-restraint, justice and, in sum, all true virtues, exist only with understanding, whether pleasures and fears and all other such things are added or taken away. But with respect to things that are separated from understanding or exchanged with each other, that sort of virtue is but painting with shadows; it is servile and has nothing healthy or true about it. For truth is a certain purification from all such things, and self-restraint, righteousness, courage, and even understanding are themselves a kind of cleansing. And these men who established the sacred rites for us are not likely to be paltry men, but merely spoke opaquely long ago, saying that he who arrives at Hades uninitiated and imperfect will lie in the mire, but he who is purified and perfected will dwell with the gods. For as they say concerning the sacred rites, "Many are the fennel-bearers, but few the bacchanals." And the latter, in my opinion, are the philosophers. (*Phaedo* 69b-d)

The Greek, φρόνησις, which can be understood as both "knowledge" and "prudence," has been consistently translated here and elsewhere in this commentary as "understanding," signifying simultaneously the theoretical and practical aspects of the intellect. Holiness and religious purity are a matter of both the theoretical and practical intellect, not the theoretical alone. It differs from ἐπιστήμη, which signifies theoretical knowledge or science. So, it is the man who devotes himself to understanding who attains holiness, and this understanding is attained only by a kind of separation of the soul from the body. Such a man would then have no fear of physical death, as Socrates explains:

> Then, as I said in the beginning, it would be ridiculous if a man who had in life prepared himself by living in a way as near as possible to having died, should then become disturbed at death. (*Phaedo* 67d-e)

... Now the man who was slain was a certain hireling of mine, and as we were farming on Naxos, he was laboring there with us...

Farming has already been established as a metaphor for education. Plato is speaking of an educational hireling, a sophist. However, the Greek used for "hireling," πελάτής, literally "one who approaches or comes near," is also a term for a suitor, one who approaches a woman. By this term Plato evokes again the analogy between the family and state and identifies this hireling as one who would usurp legitimate paternal and kingly authority, not unlike those who swarmed about Ithaca in the absence of Odysseus.

... At any rate, having become drunk and angry with a certain one of our house-slaves, he cut his throat...

Drunkenness in the dialogues signifies more than physical inebriation through wine. It indicates that the drunken individual is seeking knowledge through the changing sensation of bodies, rather than the vision of the immutable divine ideas. As Socrates explains in *Phaedo*:

> Now for a long time we have also been saying that the soul, when it uses the body to observe anything, either through seeing or hearing or any of the senses–for to observe through the body is the same thing as to observe through the senses–is dragged by the body to things ever changing, and the soul wanders about confused and becomes dizzy like a drunkard because it is fastened to such things. (*Phaedo* 79c)

Such a man is this sophist, who, lacking genuine knowledge, chases dizzily after sensible bodies. Of such a sort also is Alcibiades, a former student of Socrates, who, unable to keep his gaze fixed on the ideas becomes as changeable as the bodies he perceives, symbolized by his drunken entrance toward the close of the *Symposium*. Of Socrates, however, Alcibiades says, "And in festivities, he alone had full enjoyment of it, but even, not wishing to drink, whenever he was forced to, he outlasted everyone. But most amazing of all, not one man has ever seen Socrates drunk." (*Symposium* 220a) Plato emphasizes that the hireling had murdered a member of the house, of which the murderer himself was not a member. Through the family-state analogy he thus emphasizes that the sophists are not genuine Athenians, but foreigners, traveling from city to city making money by their labors.

... My father then bound his hands and feet, throwing him into a certain ditch, and sent a man here to inquire from the interpreter of the law what he ought to do. But during this time, he esteemed him little and did not even care for the bound man, since he was a murderer, and it was therefore no matter if he should die, which very thing in fact happened; for he died of hunger and cold and the bonds before the messenger returned from the interpreter...

Euthyphro's father bound the hands and feet of the hired farmhand and left him in a ditch. By analogy, Socrates has bound the sophist by his arguments. Now the Oedipal analogy has become more explicit. Recall that it is Oedipus who was bound and left to die by his own parents to avoid the prophecy that he would kill his father and marry his mother. Indeed, his very name, Ὀιδίπος, signifies in Greek, "he with the swollen foot," a reference to the effect of his bonds. Unlike Oedipus, this hireling did indeed die, at least figuratively, and was saved from the great evil he would have committed. Oedipus himself laments:

> Curse on the man who took
> the cruel bonds from off my legs, as I lay in the field.
> He stole me from death and saved me,
> no kindly service.
> Had I died then
> I would not be so burdensome to friends.
> (*Oedipus the King*, 1349-1355)

Euthyphro's father, a double for Socrates, just as Euthyphro is for Meletus, is cast again in the role of prudent Creon, who, having come to know the crimes of Oedipus, must now decide upon the appropriate punishment:

Oedipus:	Drive me from here with all the speed you can
	to where I may not hear a human voice.
Creon:	Be sure, I would have done this had not I
	wished first of all to learn from the god the
	course of action I should follow.
Oedipus:	But his word
	has been quite clear to let the parricide,
	the sinner, die.
Creon:	Yes, that indeed was said.
	But in the present need we had best discover
	what we should do.
	(*Oedipus the King*, 1436-1443)

Both Creon and Euthyphro's father proceed with caution, wishing to determine the religious law in such a case, in this way demonstrating their own holiness.

... Now my father and my other relatives are enraged about these things, because for the sake of this manslayer I am prosecuting for murder my own father, a man who either did not commit murder, as they say, or, if it were true that he killed him, since the man who was killed was himself a murderer, one need not take thought of such a one; for it is an unholy thing for a son to prosecute his father for murder. See how badly they know, Socrates, how the divine order holds concerning the holy and the unholy!

Euthyphro has now introduced the general matter of the divine order as it is realized in holiness and unholiness. He maintains that his relationship to his father has no bearing upon the holiness of his indictment whereas, traditionally, piety is a virtue that is owed to parents. Consequently, Euthyphro wholly ignores the pleas and arguments of his family. Again, Plato makes a reference to *Oedipus the King*:

Creon:	If you think obstinacy without wisdom
	a valuable possession, you are wrong.
Oedipus:	And you are wrong if you believe that one,
	a criminal, will not be punished only
	because he is my kinsman.
	[*Oedipus the King*, 549-552]

Now it is time for Socrates to assume his role as the winged Sphinx by quizzing Euthyphro, binding him fast until the latter solves the Socratic riddles and answers for his way of life. Indeed, as "Oedipus" (Οἰδίπος), signifies, "he with the swollen foot," so "Sphinx" is derived from σφίγγειν, which is a verb meaning "to bind fast."

Socrates: *But, in the name of Zeus, Euthyphro, do you think that you possess so accurate a knowledge concerning divine matters, of both holy and unholy things, that, when things have been done in the way you have described, you do not fear that by prosecuting your father you in turn may chance to perform an unholy deed?*

Euthyphro: *There would be no use for me, Socrates, nor would Euthyphro differ at all from the multitude of men, if I did not know accurately all such matters.*

Socrates: *Then the most excellent thing for me, wondrous Euthyphro, is to become your student, and, before the indictment, the one touching upon Meletus, to challenge him on these same things, saying that I for my part also in times past highly valued the knowledge of divinity, and that, since he says that I improvise rashly and miss the mark by innovating about divine things, I have now become your student. "And if, Meletus," I would say, "you agree that Euthyphro is wise about such matters, believe that I also acknowledge them rightly, and drop the charges. But if not, bring a charge against him, my teacher, rather than against me, for corrupting old men, both myself and his father, by teaching me and by correcting and punishing his father." And if I cannot persuade him either to drop the charge, or indict you instead of me, I could say the same things in the court that I was challenging him with.*

Since Euthyphro claims to have an exact understanding of all matters that pertain to the gods, Socrates proposes that Euthyphro become his teacher. In this manner will he be able to free himself from the accusations leveled against him. The accusation has been reversed. Meletus, through Euthyphro, will be explicitly on trial for "*corrupting old men, both myself and his father, by teaching me and by correcting and punishing his father.*" Socrates assumes the role of the accuser of Meletus and of Euthyphro simultaneously, acting in the person of their fathers. The trial has begun:

Chorus: Here comes his prosecutor:
led by your men the godly prophet comes
in whom alone of mankind truth is native.
(*Oedipus the King*, 297-299)

Euthyphro: *By Zeus, Socrates, if he should attempt to indict me, I think I would find where his weakness lies, and the argument in the court would come to be about him much sooner than about me.*

Socrates: And consequently, my friend and companion, perceiving these things, I want to become your student, knowing that neither this Meletus nor anyone else seems to notice you at all. But so keenly and so easily has he observed me that he has indicted me for impiety.

The argument in this court will indeed be more about Meletus than Euthyphro. Euthyphro conceives the question of wisdom and understanding in terms of battle, and, moreover, a public one in the courts. This is one of the skills taught by the sophists ("wise men"). Consider, on the other hand, how Socrates proposes to pursue knowledge:

Socrates: Therefore, if you and I were clever and wise, having examined thoroughly everything belonging to the mind, we might spend the remaining time making trials of each other out of our superabundance and, charging toward each other sophist-like into such a battle, smite the arguments of others with our own. However, since we are private persons, we shall wish first to contemplate things in themselves, that is, what the things being reasoned about are and whether or not they harmonize with each other. (*Theaetetus* 154d-e)

By accepting Euthyphro's boast in a very literal way, Socrates has inverted the indictment of Meletus. Before proceeding, however, Socrates takes aim at Euthyphro's lack of substance and unimportance to the state by pointing out that he is literally unknown and unobserved by Athenians, just as Socrates observed earlier about Meletus.

... So now, in the name of Zeus, tell me what you just now claimed to know so clearly. What sort of thing do you say that the pious and the impious are, concerning both murder and other things? Is not the holy itself the self-same in every action, and is not the unholy itself, the opposite of everything holy, in turn, the self-same? And whatever the unholy is to be, will it not possess a single complete idea?

Euthyphro: *Absolutely, Socrates.*

Socrates: Tell me then, what do you say the holy and unholy are?

The setting of the dialogue is complete. Socrates now turns to the primary question: What is holiness? Euthyphro, and by implication Meletus, must now answer. He must search for the Idea of the Holy. This Idea must be both "*single*": one Idea must apply to all holy actions. Moreover, it must be "*complete*": it must contain all that is necessary to identify holy actions and, presumably, nothing extraneous.

<h1 style="text-align:center">Zeus, Cronus, and Uranus</h1>

Euthyphro: Well now, I say that the holy is that which I am doing now: prosecuting a man who acts unjustly, missing the mark concerning either murder, or theft from temples, or any other such thing, whether it happens to be your father, or your mother, or anyone else. But not prosecuting is the unholy. Why, Socrates, see the great and sure sign I offer to you, one that I have described to others as well, that the law is so, and that if things happen thus, then rightly so, and moreover that one must not indulge the man who acts impiously, whoever he may be. For men acknowledge that Zeus is the best of the gods, and the most just, and yet they agree that he bound his father because the latter was unjustly swallowing his sons, and that his father, in turn, castrated his own father for other such things. But they are enraged against me, because I proceed against my father, who acts unjustly, and thus they say opposite things about the gods and about me.

Indeed, one would have to say different things about the gods and Euthyphro, for neither is he in communion with the divine Ideas, nor is he to be counted among the philosophers. Euthyphro offers his first definition of the Holy, that prosecuting the wrongdoer in the courts, regardless of one's relationship to that person, is holy and not prosecuting is unholy. He sees a religious sanction of this universal principle in the example of Zeus and his father, Cronus, as well as that of Cronus and his father, Uranus. The story is recounted by Hesiod:

> But Rhea was subject in love to Cronus and bore splendid children, Hestia, Demeter, and gold-shod Hera and strong Hades, pitiless in heart, who dwells under the earth, and the loud-crashing Earth-Shaker, and wise Zeus, father of gods and men, by whose thunder the wide earth is shaken. These great Cronus swallowed as each came forth from the womb to his mother's knees with this intent, that no other of the proud sons of heaven should hold the kingly office amongst the deathless gods. For he learned from Earth [Gaia] and starry Heaven [Uranus] that he was destined to be overcome by his own son, strong though he was, through the contriving of great Zeus. Therefore, he kept no blind outlook, but watched and swallowed down his children: and unceasing grief seized Rhea. But when she was about to bear Zeus, the father of gods and men, then she besought her own dear parents, Earth and starry Heaven, to devise some plan with her that the birth of her dear child might be concealed, and that retribution might overtake the great crafty Cronus for his own father and also for the children whom he had swallowed down. (*Theogony* 453-473)

Rhea then fooled Cronus into swallowing a great stone instead of her son, Zeus. Later, Zeus forced Cronus to release his brothers and sisters and then bound his father:

> And he set free from their deadly bonds the brothers of his father, sons of heaven whom his father in his foolishness had bound. And they remembered to be grateful to him for his

kindness, and gave him thunder and the glowing thunderbolt and lightening: for before that, huge Earth had hidden these. In them he trusts and rules over mortals and immortals. (*Theogony* 501-506)

Euthyphro conceives himself in the role of Zeus as he punishes his own father for the death of the hireling. Yet, evidently, he has failed to see that the cases are not parallel, for Zeus performed these actions on behalf of family members who had been unjustly swallowed by his father, whereas Euthyphro is prosecuting his own father for the sake of a hireling. Euthyphro has not fully understood the query of Socrates: *"But was the person killed by your father one of your relatives? But of course! For surely you would not charge him with murder for the sake of a stranger."* The example of Zeus and Cronus has thus already failed to prove the universality of Euthyphro's claim.

At this juncture one must consider Plato's attitude toward the gods, for under the veil of the popular religion he introduces a radically new theology. Gods for Plato are nothing other than ensouled divine Ideas. For example, Aphrodite is no superhuman figure, but rather the divine Idea of Pleasure, subsisting apart from pleasurable things. So says Socrates:

> We must attempt it, beginning with the very goddess who, they say, is called by the name of Aphrodite, but whose truest name is "Pleasure." (*Philebus* 12b)

Likewise, Athena, the goddess of wisdom, is Wisdom in itself. And yet the popular names do remain acceptable and pleasing to the gods:

> Yes, by Zeus, if we employ our minds, Hermogenes, there is one most beautiful manner of naming, though we know nothing of the gods, either about them or about the names by which they call themselves, whatever those may be. For it is clear that they themselves do address each other in the true manner. But there is a second correctness, from which the gods take delight in being thus named, as is the custom in the prayers we make, since we know of no other names. And this seems, at least to me, to be a beautiful custom. (*Cratylus* 400d-401a)

It can be rightfully said that Plato was saving the old pagan religion from its own absurdities and gross immoralities by translating it from a mythological to a rational basis. Plato constructed a natural theology to undergird the life of natural virtue. Whether his theology was polytheistic or monotheistic depends ultimately upon the answer to two questions. First, can the multitude of Ideas exist apart from each other, or they embraced under a single Idea? Second, what is the relationship of these many Ideas to the supervening Idea? However, these questions are beyond the scope of this commentary.

The proper relationship between father and son is certainly one of the matters Plato is examining through Cronus and Zeus, but he also insinuates a philosophical structure into the mythical origins of these gods. One must resort again to Plato's *Cratylus*, his lexicon of philosophical terms. The tongue-in-cheek etymologies made by Socrates include many of the gods. Zeus is preeminent among them:

And it appears that a name has also been laid down beautifully for his father, who is said to be Zeus, but it is not easy to understand. For the name of Zeus is artlessly something like a phrase. Dividing it in two, some of us use the one part and the others use the other. For some call him "Zena" (Ζῆνα) and other call him "Dia" (Δία). Putting them together into one reveals the nature of the god, which is just what we were asserting is proper for a name to accomplish. For there is no one at all, other than the ruler and king of all, who is the cause of life (ζῆν) for us and for all others. Therefore, this god happens to be named rightly, through whom (δι' ὃν) life (ζῆν) begins for all things that live. (*Cratylus* 395e-396b)

Socrates compares two alternate forms of the accusative case of the irregular declension of Ζεύς (Zeus), which are Ζῆνα and Δία. From these he concocts a phrase expressing Plato's conception of the god. Zeus is the bringer of life and is thus closely connected to the soul, a subject that will be investigated throughout the dialogue. Plato provides similarly playful origins for the names of both Cronus and Uranus:

To someone first hearing this, it might seem a most irreverent presumption that Zeus is the son of Cronus, but well-spoken to say that Zeus is the offspring of some great intelligence. And, indeed, Cronus (Κρόνος), signifies not child (κόρος), but the pure (καθαρὸν) and undefiled character of the mind. And this is the son of Uranus, as is passed down. But the power of looking upward is beautifully called by the name, "Urania" (οὐρανία), from looking at the things above (ὁρῶ τὰ ἄνω). (*Cratylus* 396b-c)

What is being described in mythological terms is the vision of the divine Ideas. It begins with Uranus and the looking at things above (ὁρῶ τὰ ἄνω). One turns away from the sensible toward the intelligible, that which can be apprehended only by the mind. By the begetting of Cronus is signified that the mind is made pure (καθαρὸν) of the dross of sensible images, and by the begetting in turn of Zeus is understood that the soul enters into the divine life, which is a communion with the Ideas. What then is the significance of the bonds in which Zeus (signifying the soul) places his father, Cronus (signifying the mind)? It is simply this: Knowledge transcends true opinion by a bond of reason that constrains one to maintain that something is precisely so and cannot be otherwise. The nature of this bond is only revealed later in the dialogue.

The War Between the Gods and Giants

Socrates: *Is it not for this reason, Euthyphro, that I am fleeing the indictment, namely, that whenever someone says such things about the gods, I somehow find it hard to accept, because of which, it would seem, someone will say that I missed the mark. Now then, if these things seem true to you, who know so well about such things, it is surely necessary, so it would seem, that we also yield. For what shall we say, we who agree that we know nothing concerning these things? So, tell me, in the name of Zeus, the god of friendship, do you truly believe that these things happened so?*

Socrates professes that he really knows nothing about the truth of Greek theogony, and that many will consider him to have "*missed the mark.*" Recall that Plato used *Cratylus* to identify opinion with the shooting of a bow. Erroneous opinion is then nothing other than missing the target at which one is shooting. In a feigned humility, he assumes the opinion of Euthyphro, who, he suggests, knows more by far about such matters. Moreover, Socrates preemptively undermines Euthyphro's opinion that there are wars and enmities between the gods by invoking Zeus, the highest of the Greek gods, under the title of the "*god of friendship.*" In Book II of the *Republic*, Plato voices through Socrates a severe judgment upon the relating of these very stories:

> "Yes, indeed," he said, "these are difficult sayings." "Yes, and these stories are not to be related in our city, nor are they to be told to a young man listening that in acting unjustly to the extreme he would do nothing to be marveled at, nor in punishing in every way his father who has acted unjustly but would be doing just what the first and greatest of the gods did." "No, by Zeus," he said, "it does not seem to me serviceable to speak of such things." "Nor are we ever to say that gods make war upon gods and plot against each other and fight battles." (*Republic* 377e-378b)

There is a manifest connection between the two dialogues. The *Republic* provides a clarification of the view of Socrates on such matters. Through irony, Plato manages to use these "difficult sayings," difficult because their serviceable meanings have remained hidden, even as he uses Socrates to denounce their popular understanding and import.

Euthyphro: *Yes, Socrates, and things to be wondered at more than these, which the multitude does not know.*

Socrates: *And you believe that there was really a war amongst the gods, and terrible hatreds, and battles, and many other such things, the sort told by the poets and with which the temples have been adorned in many colors by good painters—but above all the robe that is carried up to the Acropolis during the festival of the Great Panathenaea is filled with such embroideries. Shall we say that these things are true, Euthyphro?*

Socrates now queries Euthyphro about the story of the gigantomachy, the war between the Olympian gods and the giants. When Cronos castrated his father, the drops of blood fell to earth (Gaia), and she conceived the earthborn race of giants, which in later Greek history were identified with the titans. The severed genitals of Uranus fell to the sea, creating a foam out of which was engendered Aphrodite, the goddess of pleasure, or simply Pleasure. Hesiod described the war thus:

> For the Titan gods and as many as sprung from Cronos had long been fighting together in stubborn war with heart-grieving toil, the lordly titans from high Othrys, but the gods, givers of good, whom rich-haired Rhea bore in union with Cronos, from Olympus. So they, with bitter wrath, were fighting continually with one another at that time for ten full years, and the hard strife had no close or end for either side, and the issue of the war hung evenly balanced. (*Theogony* 629-638)

The giants were ultimately punished for their hubris, their willingness to transgress divine limits. The story is certainly unworthy of divinity, and Plato may indeed be presenting the condemnation made by the historical Socrates on the matter. Plato always keeps the arguments of Socrates within certain intellectual bounds, reserving for other characters the kind of high metaphysical assertions found in *Parmenides, Sophist,* or *Timaeus.* The outward concern of Socrates is that of definition, and to credit him as the originator of a rudimentary theory of the Ideas, as Plato does in *Parmenides* 128e-130b, seems entirely reasonable. However, more important than discerning the genuine attitude of Socrates in the dialogues, a task fraught with uncertainty, is understanding how Plato uses these myths to express his own doctrines, which transcend metaphysically the limited perspective of his one-time instructor. The myth of the gigantomachy becomes in the hands of Plato a potent symbol and analogy for the battle between the materialists and idealists:

Stranger: And there would indeed seem to be amongst themselves something like a battle of gods and giants on account of their dispute with each other about the essence of things.

Theaetetus: How is that?

Stranger: Some drag down to earth everything from heaven and the invisible, artlessly grasping rocks and trees with their hands; for, fastening themselves to all such things, they affirm with confidence that only that exists which can be touched and embraced, defining body and essence as the same thing. But if someone says that some existing thing is not a body, they thoroughly despise him, listening to nothing that anyone else proposes.

Theaetetus: They are terrible men whom you describe. I myself have chanced upon many of them.

Stranger: Accordingly, they who argue against them defend themselves very piously with the unseen from above, contending that true being and essence consists in intelligible but bodiless ideas. But the bodies of those other men and their so-called truth they will break down into tiny pieces in their arguments, addressing them not as essence, but as a certain generation being carried along. And both parties, Theaetetus, have joined in a boundless battle concerning these things. (*Sophist* 246a-c)

There is much to take away from this analogy. There is indeed a battle between the gods and giants, that is, between idealists and materialists, about the character of οὐσίας. This term has a twofold sense. First, it indicates a primacy of intelligibility, second, a primacy of being. Inasmuch as one wishes to assert its separation from bodies, it is best translated as "essence," but should one wish to assert its capacity to receive other corporeal perfections, to "stand under" them, "substance" is the better translation. The former is the view of the partisans of the Ideas; the latter is the view of the earthborn. A war is being waged over whether οὐσίας is identical with body, as maintained by the earthborn materialists, or identical with the divine Ideas. The materialists take even spiritual beings—the soul, truth, goodness, and indeed holiness—and make them out to be either bodies or the properties of bodies. They grasp things "artlessly" because they do not grasp them by their intellects, but by the senses. Without the knowledge that can only be attained by the mind, there can be no genuine art.

Ranged against the materialists are the idealists, who maintain that the primacy of intelligibility and being belongs to the Ideas. These ideas are bodiless, but nonetheless more real than the bodies that imitate them. The senses give no access to them; they can only be seen by the soul itself. Confronting the earthborn, partisans of the Ideas argue "piously," because they respect the divine nature of the Ideas, however that is to be construed. Finally, by the analysis of bodies and their motion, the defenders of the Ideas demonstrate that bodies are undergoing a continual generation through time, "a certain generation being carried along." Bodies are in a flux and, as such, are not the proper object of knowledge.

During the festival of the Great Panathenaea, a robe, or πέπλος, was carried up to the Acropolis, the high part of the city, and specifically to the Temple of Athena Parthenos, more commonly called the Parthenon. Upon this were embroidered such events and battles that are described by the poets. This reference may appear to have no purpose but to illustrate the importance of such stories to the state religion, but there is a good deal more to it. In Book VIII of the *Republic*, Socrates describes the democratic form of government in the following terms:

> "It may chance," I said, "to be the most beautiful of states; just as a many-colored robe embroidered with all hues, so also this state, embroidered with men of every character, would appear to be most beautiful. And perhaps," I said, "many, just like women and boys seeing multicolored objects, would indeed judge it most beautiful." (*Republic* 557c)

Plato is criticizing a very specific form of government, namely, the democratic, along with the popular mythical religion that it enshrines. Such a government may appear beautiful to uneducated "women and boys," but it is not so in fact. To understand why it is not, one must carefully consider Plato's understanding of the Beautiful (τὸ καλόν):

In my opinion, these things must first be distinguished: First, what is that which always is, having no generation? And, second, what is that which is always being generated and never is? Now the first is intuited by mind and apprehended by argument, always existing in and by itself. But the second, coming to be and then perishing, is a conjecture drawn from the unreasoning senses, and only seems to be, but never has genuine being. Now, again, everything that is generated necessarily comes to be by some cause, for it is impossible for anything to have generation without a cause. Now whenever the artificer, keeping in sight that which exists in and by itself, takes some such thing as a model and brings the potential and idea of his work to completion, that which is finished in this way will of necessity be entirely beautiful. But when he has regard for that which is generated, taking as his model the begotten, the work will not be beautiful. (*Timaeus* 27d-28b)

This lack of genuine beauty in the democratic state follows from its failure to attend to the unchanging divine model of government. And the robe carried to the Acropolis during the Great Panathenaea is the very emblem of this failure, attracting the popular eye for all its colors, thereby signifying the variety of characters and persuasions—good, evil, and indifferent—that belong to such a state and enshrining as the state religion popular myths that are often contrary to the moral law. Weaving is a Platonic metaphor for statecraft:

Stranger: But the art that governs all other arts and customs, bestowing care upon all things whatsoever belonging to the city and weaving together all things most rightly, we, compassing its power with the name belonging to the whole community, would most justly, I think, call the political art.

Young Socrates: Altogether so.

Stranger: Do we therefore desire to proceed according to the model of the art of weaving, now that all the classes in the city have become clear for us?

Young Socrates: Vehemently so.

Stranger: Then the kingly weaving, I think, must be described: what sort of thing it is, in what way he twines the yarn, and what sort of weave it yields. (*Statesman* 305e-306a)

The question of the proper form of government is thus bound up with the kind of threadwork that is described. The democratic form of government has been identified with a gaudy form of embroidery, yielding a variety of images, each in conformity with the desires of a fickle and unruly multitude, the very multitude that voted to put Socrates to death. The true goddess of democracy is not Athena (Wisdom), but Aphrodite (Pleasure).

I know that pleasure is a many-colored embroidery and, as I said, since we are beginning with her, it is fitting that we lay it to heart and examine what kind of nature she possesses. (*Philebus* 12c)

In the democratic state, each is permitted to follow his own pleasure, whether or not this conduces to his own well-being and that of the state.

Plato expounds the myth of the earthborn at great length (*Statesman* 269a-273e), explaining how there are periodic reversals in the revolutions of the cosmos, and how these reversals bring about corresponding reversals in human life. In the reign of Zeus, people are born of parents, grow from childhood to adulthood and then to senectitude, subsequently dying and being buried in the earth. However, in the opposite age, that is, during the reign of Cronus, the process is reversed. People begin to grow younger, not older. As described by the Stranger:

> First, whatever the animal happened to be, the age of each and every one of them came to a standstill, and every mortal ceased altogether to grow older. Turning about and back upon its opposite, each grew, as it were, younger and more supple. The white hairs of old men began to grow dark, and the cheeks of bearded men became smooth again, as each returned to what he was in times past. The bodies of those who had become adults, growing smoother and becoming smaller by day and by night, receded to the state of a new-born child, being made like one in both body and soul, and from there, altogether wasting away, they disappeared completely. (*Statesman* 270d-e)

The Stranger maintains a careful ambiguity throughout the myth. Nevertheless, it is not too difficult to discern that this reversal in development is not for the better. The loss of white hair, indicating a loss of maturity and wisdom, and the subsequent loss of a beard, which, as already explained, is used by Plato to indicate the presence of mind, each of these implies a mental regression. These individuals "receded to the state of a new-born child, being made like one in both body and soul." The more damning of the two for the philosopher is the reversion of the soul to a childish state. But then, from where could each succeeding generation come in the age of Cronus? The Stranger explains that people of that age were earthborn:

> It is clear, Socrates, that being begotten of each other did not belong to nature at that time, but that the earthborn race, which they say once existed, returned out of the earth, and this was related from memory by our earliest forebears, those who were nearest neighbors to the time in which the previous revolution was completed, but who grew up in the beginning of this age. They became for us the heralds of these tales, which are now disbelieved by many people, but without justification. For one must take consideration thereupon. It follows from the elderly returning to the nature of a child that from the dead also, lying in the earth, there are those who are reconstituted and raised again to life by the reversal of generation, as it was turned around to the opposite. For this reason, and out of necessity, the earthborn are engendered, and thus do the name and the tradition come about, except for such a number as God guided to another portion. (*Statesman* 271a-271c)

If indeed the whole order of life were inverted, so too would be the process of death. Whereas in the age of Zeus, men are born from mothers, age, die, and then are buried, in the age of Cronus, life begins when men are born from the earth, and progresses until they eventually return to the womb, running to their mothers as Meletus does to the state. This reversal also has a consequence for the institution of marriage:

> There were no states, nor was there possession of wives or children; for they all came to life out of the earth, remembering nothing from before. (*Statesman* 271e-272a)

The notion that Plato believed that wives and children should be held in common is based upon a misunderstanding of *Republic* 423e-424a. It is in fact merely the opinion of some of the earthborn against whom Plato is battling. Indeed, much of the *Republic* is a critique of Plato's radical contemporaries. Such morally degenerate principles are clearly repudiated by the extensive regulations for marriage detailed in *Laws* 772d-776b.

One must not read this myth of the earthborn as though it pertains to alternating periods of time. Even the shortest analysis of the myth in such terms would yield contradictions and insuperable objections. The myth's import lies in the distinction between the two reigns: Cronus reigning over the earthborn materialists, in whom there is a mental regression, and Zeus, the god of friendship, reigning over the idealists. These classes of men are by no means fixed. It is perfectly possible, at least "for such a number as God guided to another portion," that one may be translated from the reign of Cronus to that of Zeus. One may forsake purely corporeal philosophies and recognize the divine Ideas. Understood as a philosophical battle, Zeus is wholly justified in binding his father, Cronus. Or, to put it in clear terms, the genuine philosopher is wholly justified in binding the materialists through his arguments.

But to return to *Euthyphro*, what is the significance here of the origin of the earthborn and the war they wage against the idealists? Why does Plato make this detour into the gigantomachy at all? The purpose is to announce to the wide, attentive, and persistent reader that something bearing upon that intellectual controversy is to be revealed in this dialogue. To be more exact, Plato will examine the ontological foundation of the Ideas, of motion, and of soul. And he will do so with a concision that is made possible only by oblique references to the other dialogues.

Euthyphro: Not only those, Socrates, but, as I was just saying, if you wish, I will detail for you many other things concerning divine matters, things I know you will be shocked to hear.

Socrates: I would not wonder at it. But you can tell me those things some other time at leisure. Right now, try to state more clearly that which I was in fact just asking you. For you did not, my comrade, sufficiently teach me before, when I was asking about the holy, as to what it may be, but you were telling me that this thing which you are now doing happens to be holy, namely, prosecuting your father for murder.

Euthyphro: And I was speaking the truth, Socrates.

Socrates: Perhaps. But you say, Euthyphro, that many other things are also holy.

Euthyphro: For they are.

Socrates: Do you remember then that I was not asking you to teach me one or two of the many holy things, but that very aspect by which all holy things are holy? For you said that it is by one idea that unholy things are unholy, and holy things holy. Do you not remember?

Euthyphro: I do.

Socrates: So then, teach me now this idea, whatever it is, in order that I may look only to it, using it as a model by which, whenever you or anyone else does such a thing, I may say that it is holy, but if not such a thing, may deny it.

Euthyphro: Well, if you wish it in this way, Socrates, then I will say it in this way.

Socrates: Indeed, I do wish it.

In reading the English translation of Plato's text, one should not assume that Euthyphro is incapable of understanding the demand of Socrates. Nor is he consciously trying to evade it. The Greek, τὸ ὅσιον, can be rendered both concretely as "the holy thing" and abstractly as "the Holy," holiness itself. Euthyphro, for whom all being is body, attends only to the former and has forgotten that Socrates has asked him about the Idea of holiness, not for an instance of it. The relation between the two will only become clear as Plato lays out the central metaphysical conundrum of the dialogue. Euthyphro is judging bodily instances by his senses, whereas Socrates is asking him to ascend to an intellectual consideration of the Ideas:

> Once philosophy has seized their soul, the lovers of learning come to know that the soul is unartfully bound fast to the body, cleaving to it and being forced to behold beings through it as if through prison bars, rather than by itself through itself, and it flails about in complete

ignorance. Moreover, the soul discerns that the most terrible thing about the prison and its bars is that they are caused by carnal desire, so that it is most especially the accomplice in its own fettering. The lovers of learning, I say, then come to know that philosophy, having thus received the soul, gently encourages it and puts its hand to freeing it, pointing out that the perception of things through the eyes, and likewise through the ears and other senses, is full of deceit, and persuading it to withdraw from these insofar as it is not necessary to use them, but rather prescribing it to gather and collect itself unto itself, trusting in absolutely nothing but itself and through its mind whatever exists in and by itself. But should it look through the senses it should not at all judge to be true that which differs in differing things, for a thing of that sort is sensible and visible, whereas the soul itself sees the invisible and intelligible. (*Phaedo*, 82d-83b)

Euthyphro, and by extension Meletus, is "unartfully bound fast to the body, cleaving to it and being forced to behold beings through it." Philosophy has yet to seize his soul. The soul of Euthyphro is blind to "the Holy," that is, holiness in itself, because his soul has yet "to gather and collect itself unto itself."

Euthyphro: *Well now, that which is beloved of the gods is holy, but that which is not beloved is unholy.*

In advance of the rather long argument about this definition, it is appropriate to consider the difficulty in rendering into English φιλέω and its related Greek forms. The verbs φιλῶσιν and φιλεῖται have been translated as "(they) love" and "(it) is loved," respectively. However, one must always keep in mind that this love is not of the romantic or amorous sort, but rather, "friendship" (φιλία). Despite this ambiguity, other English renderings have still greater defects. For example, "(they) befriend" and "(it) is befriended" denote an initiation of friendship, not the state itself, and there are metaphysical questions that would be compromised by such a substitution. Additionally, the linking verbs in "(it) is a friend of" or "it is friendly toward" allow no clear distinction of active and passive voice. To distinguish for the reader the adjectival form, which does not possess voice in the manner of a verb, forms of φίλος have been consistently rendered as "beloved" and forms of θεόφιλος as "god-beloved." Translating φίλος as "dear" would have deviated even further from the ideal of a single English root corresponding to the Greek root, and still more connections would be lost. The contraries follow a parallel pattern. The verbs μισῶσιν and μισεῖται have been rendered "(they) hate" and "(it) is hated," respectively. The adjective θεομισής has been rendered "god-hated." Finally, the Greek adjective ἐχθρός has been translated substantively as "enemy" to preserve the connection with other uses in the dialogue.

Note well that this definition of Euthyphro, "that which is beloved of the gods is holy, but that which is not beloved is unholy," divides all things into two groups, with an excluded middle. The unholy consists not in a contrary quality or character, but rather the simple lack or privation of the Holy. This leaves open the possibility, subsequently examined, that there may be actions that pertain neither to holiness nor to unholiness.

One should mark here another allusion to *Oedipus the King*. Discovering that he has killed his father and married his mother, Oedipus seeks to be exiled from Thebes. He begs this favor of Creon, who wishes to consult the wishes of the gods:

Oedipus:	Do you know on what condition I obey?
Creon:	You tell me them,
	and I shall know them when I hear.
Oedipus:	That you shall send me out
	to live away from Thebes.
Creon:	That gift you must ask of the god.
Oedipus:	But now I'm hated by the gods.
Creon:	So quickly you'll obtain your prayer.
	(*Oedipus the King*, 1517-1519)

The irony and humor of Creon's reply cannot be missed. Because Oedipus is hated by the gods, his prayer to the gods for exile will be answered. There is in this a subtle suggestion that the gods think that Oedipus should not be exiled but put to death. Diogenes Laertius (*Lives of the Eminent Philosophers* 2.43) records that the Athenian people so regretted the death of Socrates, that they later put Meletus to death for his primary role in the trial. Thus, Meletus is once again the impious, unholy, and god-hated Oedipus, displayed through the character of Euthyphro.

Socrates: *You have now answered beautifully, and just as I was requiring you to answer. However, I do not yet know if this is true, but, clearly, you will go on and teach in full that the things you say are true.*

Euthyphro: *Surely.*

The reader of Plato's dialogues will likely be struck by how Socrates often praises his interlocutors for answering "beautifully." The translator might presume to correct this, by changing it to "rightly" or "correctly" or "truthfully," or might give a varied translation to break the monotony. This, however, would be to lose sight of Plato's entire meaning, which is that the speaker has crafted his speech with his mind directed toward an archetypal Idea, and that his response is a faithful image in words of that Idea. Euthyphro has now begun to turn his mind away from the holy things perceived through the senses and toward Holiness itself. It remains to determine to what extent and in what manner his answer conforms to that Idea.

Socrates: *Carry on then. Let us examine what we are saying. The god-beloved thing and the god-beloved person are holy, but the god-hated thing and the god-hated person are unholy. They are not the same, but the holy is most opposite to the unholy. Is it not so?*

Euthyphro: *It is just so.*

Socrates: *And this seems to be stated well?*

Euthyphro: *I think so, Socrates.*

Socrates: *Well then, has this also been said, that the gods quarrel and differ with each other and that there are enmities in them for each other? Has this also been said?*

Euthyphro: *It has been said.*

The question now becomes that of the gods and their relationships. According to the popular religion, the giants and Olympian gods warred against each other. If so, then they must have disagreed and quarreled about something. The subject of such disagreements may give rise to an understanding of the loves and hatreds of the gods, in keeping with the argument. For Plato's gods, the divine Ideas, there can be no such violent disagreement, only distinctions. However, among those with at least the reputation of being philosophers, there are disagreements between the idealists and earthborn materialists. As explained, Plato accepts this account as a figure of an ongoing philosophical war.

Socrates: *And concerning what things, best of men, do disagreements produce enmity and rage? Let us examine it in this way. If you and I were to differ concerning number, as to which one was more, would these differences make us enemies and cause us to rage against each other, or rather, by resorting to counting in such matters, would we not be quickly reconciled?*

Euthyphro: *Certainly.*

Socrates: *And so, therefore, if we were to disagree concerning the greater and lesser, would we put an end to the disagreement by resorting to measurement?*

Euthyphro: *It is just so.*

Socrates: *And, by recourse to weighing, I think, we would settle our dispute concerning the heavier and lighter.*

Euthyphro: *How otherwise?*

Plato now introduces an analogy. If in doubt about number, magnitude, or weight, one would simply draw from the sciences of number, measure, and weight. If in doubt about number, count it; if in doubt about length, measure it; if in doubt about weight, place it in the balance. In each case there are rational standards of judgment, which obviate the need to engage in violent conflict. Plato will make use of this analogy later in the dialogue.

Socrates: But having differed about what, being unable to come to any judgment, would we be enemies and rage against each other? Perhaps the answer is not really at hand for you. But, as I speak, see if these things are the just and unjust, the beautiful and shameful, and the good and evil. Are not these the things about which, having differed and being yet unable to come to a satisfactory judgment, we become enemies to each other, when we do in fact become enemies, both you, and I, and all other men?

Euthyphro: Yes, these are the differences, Socrates. It concerns these things.

Socrates: Well? Would not the gods, Euthyphro, if in fact they do differ, differ on account of these things?

Euthyphro: It is a great necessity.

Socrates now questions Euthyphro about the kinds of things concerning which one would become enemies: "*the just and unjust, the beautiful and shameful, and the good and evil.*" Note the parallel with number, measure, and weight.

Socrates: And so, noble-born Euthyphro, according to your argument, some of the gods think that some things are just and unjust, and beautiful and shameful, and good and evil, but others think otherwise; for they would not in any way be quarreling with each other if they did not differ concerning these things? Is it so?

Euthyphro: You speak correctly.

Socrates: Therefore, the things which each group thinks are in fact beautiful and good and just, these things they love, but the things opposite to these they hate?

Euthyphro: Certainly.

Socrates: But these things, as you say, some think just, but others unjust. And disputing about these things they quarrel and wage war against each other. Is it not so?

Euthyphro: It is so.

Euthyphro answers that, indeed, these are things about which not only men disagree, but the gods as well, leading to violent conflicts. Implicit in Euthyphro's admission is the belief that these matters of disagreement cannot be adjudicated by a rational standard of judgment, but must remain matters of opinion, dependent upon the senses. Such, in Plato's view, is the situation for the materialist.

Socrates: *Then the same things, it would seem, are hated and loved by the gods, and the god-hated and god-beloved would be the same.*

Euthyphro: *It would seem so.*

Socrates: *And then holy things and unholy things would be the same, Euthyphro, by this argument.*

Euthyphro: *There is that possibility.*

Socrates: *Then you did not answer what I was asking, wondrous man. For I did not ask what one thing happens to be both holy and unholy, but it would seem that what is god-beloved is also god-hated. The result, Euthyphro, is that, with regard to what you are now doing, punishing your father, it would not be wondered at if doing this makes you beloved of Zeus, but an enemy to Cronos and Uranus, and beloved of Hephaestus, but an enemy to Hera. And if any one of the gods differs with another about the same, it will be the same for them too.*

Euthyphro's second attempt at defining holiness has failed. Socrates now points out clearly that if what is loved by the gods is also hated by the gods, then, according to the definition of Euthyphro, holy things and unholy things would be identical. So, in punishing his father, he may be pleasing to Zeus, who punished his own father, but displeasing to Cronos and Uranus, the father and grandfather of Zeus. The second reference requires some background. After Zeus begot Athena, the goddess of Wisdom, without a mother, Hera then conceived without Zeus her own son, Hephaestus:

> "But Hera without union with Zeus – for she was very angry and quarreled with her mate – bore famous Hephaestus, who is skilled in crafts more than all the sons of Heaven." (Hesiod, *Theogony*, 927-929)

Hephaestus, though skilled in the art of metalworking, was badly deformed. He was often portrayed by Greek artists as having his feet facing backwards. Hera, horrified and shamed by her conception, cast from heaven Hephaestus, who then fell to the sea.

> "Hear from me, all gods and goddesses, how cloud-gathering Zeus begins to dishonor me wantonly, when he has made me his true-hearted wife. See now, apart from me he has given birth to bright-eyed Athena, who is foremost among all the blessed gods. But my son, Hephaestus, whom I bore was weakly among all the blessed gods and shriveled of foot, a shame and disgrace to me in heaven, whom I myself took in my hand and cast out so that he fell in the great sea." (*Homeric Hymn: To Pythian Apollo*, 311-318)

Hera, the mother, signifies the state. Hephaestus is a figure for Meletus, who was conceived by the Athenian state while the populace quarreled with the genuine philosopher-kings, represented by Zeus. Meletus is morally deformed, and is consequently cast forth by the state itself out of shame for killing Socrates. Euthyphro may be pleasing to such a one, but not to the state.

Euthyphro: *But I think, Socrates, that concerning this at least, namely, that he who kills someone unjustly ought not to pay the penalty, not one of the gods differs, the one with the other.*

Socrates: *Well? Of men at least, Euthyphro, have you ever heard of anyone disputing that he who had killed unjustly, or had done anything else at all unjustly, ought not to pay the penalty?*

Euthyphro: *They never cease to dispute these things, both in the courts and elsewhere. For those who act unjustly in all such cases will say and do anything when fleeing a charge.*

Socrates: *But do they agree, Euthyphro, that they act unjustly and, thus agreeing, nevertheless say that they ought not to pay the penalty?*

Euthyphro: *In no way do they say that!*

Socrates: *Then, at least, they do not do and say everything. For I think they do not dare to say or dispute, that if they in fact act unjustly, the penalty need not be paid; but I think they deny that they act unjustly. Is it not so?*

Euthyphro: *You speak the truth.*

Socrates: *Then they do not, at least, dispute that the one acting unjustly ought not to pay the penalty. But perhaps they dispute about who is the one acting unjustly, and what he has done, and when.*

Euthyphro: *True indeed.*

Socrates: *Then even the gods have suffered the same, if in fact they quarrel concerning things just and unjust, as is your argument, and some affirm that others have acted unjustly, but some deny it? Since surely, wondrous man, no one, either of the gods or of men, dares to say that the penalty need not be paid by the one acting unjustly.*

Euthyphro: *Yes. You speak the truth, Socrates, in the main.*

Socrates speaks the truth "in the main," for there is an exception. There is indeed someone who maintains that one who acts unjustly ought not always to be punished: Socrates himself. This is precisely his argument to Meletus in Plato's *Apology*:

Of these things I am not persuaded by you, Meletus, nor do I think that anyone else is. But either I do not corrupt [the youth], or if I do corrupt, I do so involuntarily, with the result that you are lying on either account. And if I corrupt involuntarily, the law for such involuntary missing of the mark is not to drag them here [into the court], but, taking them in private, to teach them and instruct their minds. For, clearly, once I am acquainted with the matter, I will stop doing what I do involuntarily. But you fled from associating with me and teaching me, being unwilling to do so. Instead, you drag me here, where the law is to drag those requiring punishment, not learning. (*Apology* 25e-26a)

There are some who perform unjust actions involuntarily, specifically, those who act out of ignorance of the nature of justice, and these are not to be prosecuted, but instructed. On the other hand, those who perform unjust acts voluntarily, ought to be both prosecuted and punished. It is sometimes maintained by interpreters that Plato genuinely believed that anyone who knew what his good consisted in would never commit evil willingly. This opinion, stemming from a failure to perceive the irony employed by Socrates against the sophists, is repudiated in the preceding passage. The distinction between the compulsory and the voluntary is elaborated in *Cratylus*:

> **Hermogenes:** You seem to me to be racing through things.
>
> **Socrates:** Yes, for I can already see the end! But then I still wish to finish "compulsion" (ἀνάγκη) and "the voluntary" (τὸ ἑκούσιον), because these are next in line. As regards "the voluntary" (τὸ ἑκούσιον), giving way (εἶκον) and not repelling belong to the name, but, as I say, giving way to a motion happening in accordance with the will. "The compulsory" (τὸ ἀναγκαῖον) and the resistant, running counter to the will, concern error and lack of learning, and are likened to traveling through winding ravines (ἀγκή), because, a ravine, being scarcely passable, jagged, and overgrown, restrains one's motion. (*Cratylus* 420d-e)

Compulsory deeds can derive from lack of knowledge, which falsifies either the end to which one believes oneself to be acting or the means of its attainment, and thus run counter to the will. Voluntary action is simply action that is in conformity with that will. However, neither of these guarantees the rectitude of the will itself.

Socrates: But I think, Euthyphro, that the ones disputing, both gods and men, if in fact the gods do dispute, dispute each of the things that have been done. Differing about a certain action, some say that it has been done justly, but others say unjustly. Is it not so?

Euthyphro: Certainly.

Socrates: Come now, Euthyphro, my friend, teach me also, in order that I may become wiser, what evidence you have that all the gods think that the man was killed unjustly, who, being guilty of manslaughter while acting as a laborer, and having been bound by the master of the man who was killed, died on account of the bonds before he who bound him learned by inquiring of the legal interpreters what he must do about the matter, and, moreover, that for the sake of such a man it really is right that the son proceed against his father, prosecuting him for murder. Come, try to show me clearly about this, that all the gods think more than anything that it is right to do this. And if you show it sufficiently to me, I will never cease to praise you for your wisdom.

Euthyphro: But perhaps it is not a small task, Socrates, although certainly I could show it to you clearly.

Socrates now asks Euthyphro to argue in his own defense in his action against his father, but without a correct understanding of holiness in itself, Euthyphro is incapable of doing so.

Socrates: I am beginning to understand. It is because I seem to you less able to learn than the jurors; since it is clear that you will show them that these things are unjust and that all the gods together hate such things.

Euthyphro: Very clearly, Socrates, if they do indeed listen to me speak.

Socrates: But they will listen, so long as you seem to speak well...

Socrates clearly believes that the jurors in the courts are moved primarily by appearances and specious emotional appeals.

... But I thought this while you were speaking, and I am considering it with regard to myself. If Euthyphro were to teach me that all the gods think that such a death is unjust, what more have I learned from Euthyphro, as to what the holy and the unholy are? For this work, so it seems, would be god-hated. But just now it was shown that the holy and what is not holy are not defined in this way; for that which is god-beloved appeared to be also that which is god-hated, with the result that I let you off from this, Euthyphro. If you wish, let all the gods think it unjust and hate it. Shall we now amend the definition, that whatever all the gods hate is unholy and whatever they all love is holy, but what some love and others hate is neither or both? Do you wish to define the holy and the unholy in this way now?

Euthyphro: For what hinders, Socrates?

Socrates: Nothing on my part, Euthyphro, but examine your own, whether in thus proposing it you will easily teach me what you promised.

Euthyphro: Well, I would say that this is the holy, namely, that which all the gods love, and the opposite, that which all the gods hate, is the unholy.

Socrates: Shall we therefore, Euthyphro, examine again whether this is beautifully said, or shall we let it be, and accept it in this way, from both ourselves and others, if someone were merely to assert that the matter stands thus, conceding that it does? Must what the speaker says be examined?

Euthyphro: It must be examined. Yet I for my part think that it has now been defined beautifully.

At the suggestion of Socrates, Euthyphro now amends his definition of holiness to exclude whatever actions the gods cannot agree upon. In his third definition the Holy consists in what all the gods love, and the unholy in what all the gods hate.

Socrates: Good man, we shall soon know better, for I had in mind such a thing: Is the holy loved by the gods because it is holy, or is it holy because it is loved?

Euthyphro: I don't know what you mean, Socrates.

Socrates: Then I shall try to speak more clearly. We say that there is something being carried and something carrying, something being led and something leading, something being seen and something seeing. Do you begin to understand with regard to all such things that they do differ from each other, and in what manner they differ?

Euthyphro: I am beginning to understand, or at least it seems to me.

With Euthyphro's definition of the Holy emended to escape the contradictions introduced by Greek theogony, the dialogue enters its crucial phase. The decisive question is whether the Holy is loved by the gods because it is holy, or it is holy because it is loved by the gods. This question, known as the "Euthyphro Dilemma," retains its relevance today in debates between voluntarist and intellectualist theories of morality: Is the moral law subsequent to the election of divine will, or does the divine will simply impose a pre-existing and unalterable morality? The question demands many distinctions before it can even be addressed. Yet, however important this question may be to the Christian theologian, it is critical to the project of understanding *Euthyphro* that one put aside such interests until Plato's own doctrine is properly examined.

Euthyphro's failure to understand the meaning of the question allows Socrates to launch into deep metaphysical waters, into the study of being itself. Plato puts into the mouth of Socrates the grammatical distinction between the active and passive voice. In the active voice the subject of a sentence acts and in the passive voice the subject is acted upon. No one with any training in grammar will doubt the distinction. As knowledge of the world is expressed through language, it is plausible, even likely, that there be some foundation in reality for this grammatical distinction. Here it becomes important to understand that metaphysical speculation among the Greek philosophers was quite often grounded in the arts of language and mathematics. They inherited no abstract metaphysical treatises. They were rather the first, at least in the West, to produce them. It is for this reason that in *Republic 527-534*, Plato sets forth the liberal arts as the pathways to a higher wisdom. The mastery of these disciplines is a prerequisite to engaging in philosophy.

Socrates draws the distinction between that which is carried and that which carries, between that which is led and that which leads, and between that which is seen and that which sees. Though he might have exhibited the distinction by any verb possessing both an active and passive voice, Plato's choice of verbs was by no means arbitrary. Each expresses a predicate of the soul. What is important to grasp in the present context is that active and passive are common to all of them. This common distinction transcends the particulars of any given action or passion on the part of real subjects. Plato, through the mouth of the Stranger in the *Sophist*, defines "being" as follows:

> Well, I say that if anything possesses by nature any power of any kind, either to make another become something, or to suffer even the smallest thing from the slightest agent, even if only once, then this thing altogether exists. For I am setting for myself a definition that defines being as nothing other than power. (*Sophist* 247d-e)

The question of action and passion raised by Socrates at this juncture of the argument is no mere grammatical distinction. It is really about the nature of being itself and the various kinds of beings in the world. What is it that genuinely exists, and how? One ought not to underestimate the importance of Plato's definition, for it comes through Aristotle and Aquinas down to the present age in the claim that being is divided into act (ἐνέργεια, *actus*) and potency (δύναμις, *potentia*). It is fundamental to traditional philosophy.

Action and passion, acting and being acted upon, are not distinguished by some difference in formal content. The distinction is literally metaphysical, beyond the physical. This ontological character is explored by Socrates and Polus in *Gorgias*:

> **Socrates:** Then examine this: If someone does something, is it necessary that there be something suffering from the one doing it?
>
> **Polus:** It seems so to me, Socrates.
>
> **Socrates:** And does it suffer that which the one doing does? And is it of such a sort as the one doing does? I am saying something like this: If someone strikes, is it necessary that something be struck?
>
> **Polus:** Necessarily.
>
> **Socrates:** And if the one striking strikes violently or quickly, is the thing being struck also struck in this way?
>
> **Polus:** Yes.
>
> **Socrates:** Is then the suffering of the thing being struck of the same sort as what the one striking does?
>
> **Polus:** Very much so.
>
> **Socrates:** And, therefore, if someone burns, it is necessary that something be burnt?
>
> **Polus:** How otherwise?
>
> **Socrates:** And if he burns violently and painfully, the thing being burnt is burnt exactly as the one burning burns it?
>
> **Polus:** Quite so.
>
> **Socrates:** And, therefore, if someone cuts, the same explanation? For something is cut.
>
> **Polus:** Yes.

Socrates: And if the cut is large or deep or painful, the cut that is cut in the thing being cut is of such a sort as the one cutting makes the cut?

Polus: It appears so.

Socrates: Then see if you agree that what I just said is collectively true about all things: the thing suffering suffers the same sort of thing as the thing doing does.

Polus: It necessarily suffers thus. (*Gorgias* 476b-476d)

The choice of cutting (surgery) and burning (cauterization) refer to the art of the physician. Plato's concern here, as elsewhere, is with the physician of the soul. For Plato, action and passion always appear together as a pair indistinguishable in form. Every passion implies a concomitant action. Moreover, every action implies a concomitant passion. It is in this latter implication that Plato differs with Aristotle, yielding quite different conceptions of both passion and motion.

⧫

Active, Passive, and Middle Voice

Socrates: *There is also, therefore, something being loved, and the thing loving is other than this?*

Euthyphro: *How otherwise?*

Plato now extends the distinction between passion and action to the thing being loved and the thing loving, because Euthyphro's third definition is that the holy is that which is loved by all the gods.

Socrates: *Tell me now, whether the thing being carried is a thing being carried because it is carried, or on account of something else.*

Euthyphro: *No, on that account.*

Socrates: *And the thing being led because it is led, and the thing being seen because it is seen?*

Euthyphro: *Certainly.*

Socrates: *Not then because it is a thing being seen, on account of this is it seen, but conversely, because it is seen, on account of this a thing being seen; nor because it is a thing being led, on account of this is it led, but because it is led, on account of this a thing being led; nor because it is a thing being carried is it carried, but because it is carried, a thing being carried. Is that which I wish to say becoming clearer, Euthyphro? I wish to say this: that if something is generated or undergoes something, not because it is a thing being generated is it generated, but because it is generated, it is a thing being generated; nor because it is a thing undergoing, does it undergo, but because it undergoes it is a thing undergoing; or do you not agree?*

Euthyphro: *I do agree.*

At this juncture, Plato makes a subtle, but critical, substitution. He no longer compares the thing acting with the thing being acted upon, that it to say, the active with the passive. Rather, he compares being acted upon with the thing being acted upon. For example, he does not say, "Not then because it is a thing being seen does something see it," but, "Not then because it is a thing being seen, on this account is it seen." Many translators assume that the two renderings are equivalent. Because Plato had just introduced the distinction between the active and passive voices, they assume that what follows can be fully understood in those terms, but it cannot. In addition to the active and passive voices of English, Greek has a middle voice. If the present active infinitive is "to see," and the passive "to be seen," then the middle voice is "to cause to be seen." In many tense and mood combinations Greek verbs have the same form in both the passive and middle voices. This allows Plato to say two very different things simultaneously. The ontological key to the whole dialogue, indeed, to Plato's whole doctrine of ensouled Ideas, derives from this equivocation which cannot be preserved in English. The common practice of translating Plato's seemingly awkward and unnecessary passive constructions into the active voice obscures the wordplay and ultimately prevents the inference that Plato wishes the reader to make. There are in fact four possible readings of the causal relationship, in each case a statement together with its converse:

1. Not *because it is a thing being seen, on account of this is it seen,*
   but *because it is seen, on account of this it is a thing being seen.*

The first renders both the participle and verb in the passive. The claim of Socrates makes perfect sense when read in this way, for the first italicized causal relation is false, the second true. That which is seen is only a thing being seen insofar as it is seen. It does not possess this character of itself. It passively receives the action, and action is the cause of passion. One must assent to such a proposition.

2. Not *because it is a thing causing to be seen, on account of this is it seen,*
   but *because it is seen, on account of this it is a thing causing to be seen.*

The second renders the participle in the middle voice and the verb in the passive. Here, the first italicized causal relation is true and the second false. If read in this way, the statement of Socrates is not true. The effect arises from the cause, not the cause from the effect.

3. Not *because it is a thing causing to be seen, on account of this it causes to be seen,*
   but *because it causes to be seen, on account of this it is a thing causing to be seen.*

The third renders both the participle and verb in the middle voice. The first italicized causal relation is true. Something causes to be seen only if it already possesses such a power as to act as a cause. The second italicized causal relation is false. The power does not proceed from its exercise, but the exercise from the power. In accordance with this rendering, the statement of Socrates is again false.

4. Not *because it is a thing being seen, on account of this it causes to be seen,*
   but *because it causes to be seen, on account of this it is a thing being seen.*

This fourth renders the participle in the passive and the verb in the middle voice. The first causal relation is false, because the cause must precede the effect. The second italicized causal relation is true. The thing that causes to be seen can be the proper object of seeing. Thus rendered, one may assent to the proposition Socrates makes.

Socrates: *And so also the thing being loved is by this either something being generated or undergoing something?*

Euthyphro: *Certainly.*

Socrates: *And does this hold in the same way the previous cases do? Not because it is a thing being loved is it loved by those by whom it is loved, but because it is loved it is a thing being loved.*

Euthyphro: *Necessarily.*

Through Socrates Plato now applies the same distinction to the action of loving and the passion of being loved. However, the ambivalent expression once again has two English translations to which one may give assent, because the causal connection is correct:

1. Not *because it is a thing being loved is it loved* by those by whom it is loved, but *because it is loved it is a thing being loved.*

4. Not *because it is a thing being loved does it cause to be loved* by those by whom it is loved, but *because it causes to be loved it is a thing being loved.*

Likewise, there are two renderings in which assent can only be given to their converses, because the causal order is reversed:

2. Not *because it is a thing causing to be loved is it loved* by those by whom it is loved, but *because it is loved it is a thing causing to be loved.*

3. Not *because it is a thing causing to be loved does it cause to be loved* by those by whom it is loved, but *because it causes to be loved it is a thing causing to be loved.*

Euthyphro only grasps the very first of the four readings. One may also assent individually to each of the following causal relations:

a. *It is a thing being loved because it is loved.*
   (Acting is prior to being acted upon.)

b. *It is a thing being loved because it causes to be loved.*
   (An object being acted upon *may* be the cause of its being acted upon.)

c. *It is loved because it is a thing causing to be loved.*
   (An object *may be* acted upon because it causes itself to be acted upon.)

d. *It causes to be loved because it is a thing causing to be loved.*
   (Power is prior to its exercise.)

There is a hierarchy of implication among these assertions:

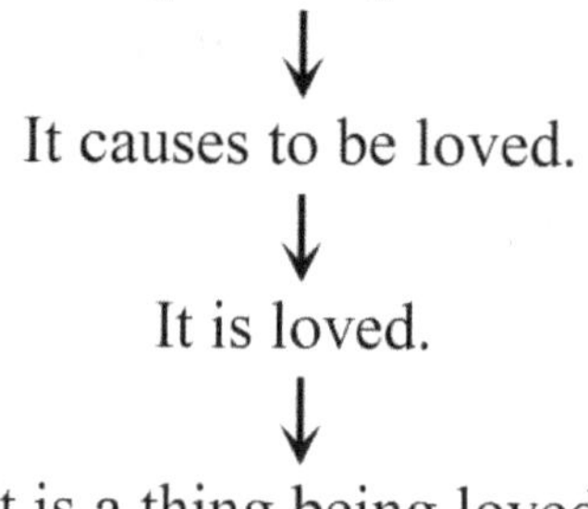

Socrates: What then do we say concerning the holy, Euthyphro? Is it loved by all the gods according to your argument?

Euthyphro: Yes.

Socrates: On account of this, that it is a holy thing, or on account of something else?

Euthyphro: No, but on account of this.

Socrates: It is loved because it is a holy thing; not because it is loved, on account of this is it a holy thing?

Euthyphro: It would seem so.

Socrates proposes that the Holy is loved by all the gods because it is holy; the Holy is not holy because it is loved by all the gods. Euthyphro gives his assent.

Socrates: But the god-beloved is the god-beloved and a thing being loved because it is loved by the gods.

Euthyphro: How otherwise?

Socrates proceeds to contrast this with the god-beloved, or, that which is loved by the gods. He is arguing against Euthyphro's own understanding, using the first reading of the equivocation in which both verb and participle are understood to be in the passive voice. The god-beloved is not loved by the gods because it is god-beloved. Rather, it is god-beloved because it is loved by the gods:

Socrates: Then the god-beloved is not the holy, Euthyphro, nor is the holy the god-beloved, as you say, but the former differs from the latter in this respect.

Euthyphro: How so, Socrates?

Socrates: Because we agree that the holy is loved on account of this, that it is holy, but it is not holy because it is loved. Do we not?

Euthyphro: Yes.

Socrates: *But we agree that the god-beloved, because it is loved by the gods, is, by this very passion of being loved, god-beloved, but not because it is god-beloved, on account of this is it loved.*

Euthyphro: *Truly spoken.*

Socrates concludes from this that the holy and the god-beloved are not the same, for the holy is loved by the gods because it is holy, but the god-beloved is the god-beloved because it is loved by the gods. The causal determination is reversed in the two cases. This distinction undermines Euthyphro's definition.

Socrates: *But if, my friend, Euthyphro, the god-beloved and the holy were the same thing, then if on the one hand the holy were loved on account of being holy, the god-beloved would also be loved on account of being the god-beloved, but if the god-beloved were the god-beloved on account of being loved by the gods, the holy would also be holy on account of being loved. But now you see that it holds conversely, and that the one is altogether different from the other. For the one has the character of being loved only because it is loved; but the other has the character of being loved, and only on account of this is it loved. And you run the risk, Euthyphro, when asked what the holy is, of not wishing to make clear to me its essence, but rather describing something which it has undergone, something the holy has suffered, specifically, to be loved by all the gods. But what it is you have not yet said. So, if this is something beloved of you, do not hide it away from me, but tell me again from the beginning: What is holiness, no matter if it is loved by the gods or if it undergoes something? Concerning this we shall not be set at odds, but speak straightforwardly, what are the holy and the unholy?*

Socrates explains that the god-beloved and the Holy cannot be substituted for each other without contradiction. Such mutual substitution is the mark of every definition. Moreover, being loved by the gods, a passion, appears to be something accidental to the Holy. He harps on the inadequacy of mere passion or suffering to define the essential being of the Holiness. The Holy is acted upon by being loved but would remain the Holy were it loved or not. Socrates then engages in some humor by suggesting that if Euthyphro truly loves the Holy and is one of the gods, that is, one of the true philosophers, he ought not to hide the truth. Socrates concludes his appeal by alluding once again to the importance of rational discussion, so that they may not become enemies to one another, as Euthyphro suggests the gods themselves are, one to another. The grammatical solution of Euthyphro's dilemma should be clear from the discussion of the middle voice. The difficulty arises because in readings 1 and 4 the first statement is false, and the converse is true. To reconcile the Holy with what is loved by all the gods, one must choose a reading in which the first statement is true and the second false. Both readings 2 and 3 satisfy this demand.

The argument is left in merely apparent contradiction. This is characteristic of many of the arguments which Socrates makes in the dialogues. Plato demands that his readers themselves correct or finish the arguments. Can the relationship between the gods and holiness be restored in a satisfactory manner? Indeed, it can, and this reveals the whole ontological foundation of Plato's doctrine of the divine Ideas. Plato's elaboration of the dilemma in the passive voice, rather than in a combination of active and passive voice, yields a text far more convoluted than would seem to be necessary. This indicates that something more is involved, specifically the use of the middle voice. To grasp its importance, one must first consider the doctrine of Ideas and the difficult questions that arise in conjunction with it. The notion that there are Ideas separate from material bodies appears to have been an innovation of Socrates. Material bodies are understood to be the images of these Ideas, and so it is necessary to understand what is meant by an image:

> **Socrates:** Perhaps what you say would be so of as many things as must be of a certain number, or else not at all be, just as ten itself, if you take away or add to it, becomes straightaway something else. But this is not the same correctness that belongs to something of a certain quality or to an image generally. Rather, the opposite, as an image is bound to not reproduce altogether every quality of the thing it images, if it is indeed destined to be an image. See if what I say is so. Would there be two such things, for example, Cratylus and the image of Cratylus, if some one of the gods not only copied your color and figure, as do scene-painters, but also made all things within of such a sort as your very own, if he should reproduce the very suppleness and warmth, the motion and life and understanding, of the sort as have been put into you, and, in a word, set down by your side all other such things as you possess? Would there be in this case Cratylus and an image of Cratylus, or two Cratyluses?
>
> **Cratylus:** There would appear to me, Socrates, to be two Cratyluses.
>
> **Socrates:** Do you see then, friend, that it is necessary to seek out another correctness of images and of the things we were just describing, and not to require, should something be lacking or superadded, that the same is no longer an image? (*Cratylus* 432a-d)

An image is not bound to be an exact replica of an Idea. Indeed, were it identical in every respect, it would be indistinguishable from the Idea itself, just as an image of Cratylus that replicated every possible feature of Cratylus would no longer be an image, but a second Cratylus. And yet this creates a very serious objection to the theory of Ideas. Parmenides, in the dialogue named for him, raises a potent objection to the theory of Socrates:

> "And this argument does not hold, Parmenides," [Socrates] said, "but this most especially appears to hold, that these Ideas stand in nature as patterns, and these other things imitate

them and are likenesses of them. And this participation in the Ideas turns out to be nothing other than being the images of them." "Then," [Parmenides] said, "if anything is like the Idea, is that Idea of such a sort as to be unlike the image being made of it, inasmuch as the latter has been made like it? Or is there some contrivance that the like is unlike its like?" "There is none." "But is there not a great necessity that the like participate in the same Idea as its like?" "There is a necessity." "And is it not by participation in the Idea itself that like things are like?" "Altogether so." "Then there is nothing that is like the Idea, nor is the Idea like anything else. Otherwise, another Idea will always appear beside the first, and if that were similar to it, again another, and the generation of another Idea will never stop, that is, if the Idea were like the thing participating it." "That is very true." "Then it is not by likeness that other things partake of the ideas, but one must seek something else by which they partake." "It would seem so." (*Parmenides* 132c-133a)

Socrates maintains that the participation by which things share in the same Idea consists in their being so many likenesses of it. Parmenides then argues that if participation in the Ideas is by similitude, the Idea and its image could only be similar to each other by participating in another Idea, to which each would bear a relation of similarity. For although the instance can be similar to the Idea by participation, the Idea, which is therefore likewise similar to the instance, cannot be so by participation. Both would therefore have to be images of a second Idea. But then these two images would be similar to the second Idea, and in turn, the second idea would be similar to each of these. This, in turn, would demand a third Idea, and so on. By such a participation there could be no end of the Ideas, and therefore no first Idea in which all likenesses would participate.

This argument has come down to us through Aristotle as the "third man" argument: If there is an essential Idea of man separate from the individual instance of Socrates, an Idea in which Socrates participates, then there must be a third man in which both Socrates and the essence of man participate. Aristotle's argument is, however, derived from Plato, who upheld the Ideas. What for Aristotle is an argument against the Ideas *tout court* is for Plato merely an objection to a particular theory of Ideas. Moreover, the solution to this difficulty raised in *Parmenides*, one of the "late" dialogues, so called, is found in *Euthyphro*, one of the so-called "early" dialogues.

To speak to the dialogue, if holy things do not participate in the Holy by similitude, then how do they participate? The answer clearly lies in the discussion about the active, passive, and middle voices in ancient Greek. The Greek, φιλεῖται, means both "(it) is loved" and "(it) causes to be loved." Likewise, φιλούμενον, means both "a thing being loved" and "a thing causing to be loved." The forms of the present indicative verb and present participle are the same in both the passive and middle voice. Recall as well that the Holy (τὸ ὅσιον), taken abstractly as holiness, has the same form as its bodily instance, the holy thing (τὸ ὅσιον). Turning to the order of knowledge, the Holy is distinguished from the holy thing by its "causing to be known." In this way it possesses the perfection necessary to be an object of knowledge, rather than opinion. The Holy is known (passive voice) and causes to be known (middle voice). The instance is known (passive voice) but does not possess the perfection of causing-to-be-known (middle voice), except by recourse to the Idea.

The bodily instance is not an image of the Idea by virtue of a relation of similitude. This relation is not primarily morphological, even if that relation of similitude exists. Rather, the Idea stands above the instance by virtue of its more perfect ontological character. Whereas bodies are capable of only acting and being acted upon, the Idea admits acting, being acted upon, and causing to be acted upon. Bodies in themselves therefore lack the essential cause of knowledge. The Ideas are the proper, primary, and perfect objects of knowledge. No further Idea is required. Be that as it may, Plato's doctrine of Ideas should not be construed as implying that material instances of the Ideas are unknowable, only that they are unknowable *per se*. They can be known, but only when brought under an Idea. The Idea is in itself a stable object of the understanding. and when bound with a sensible body, it makes the body to be stably understood. It is for this reason that Plato has Socrates demand of his interlocutors that they be able to define a virtue before they can practice it. For if they have no knowledge of the Idea, then they can have no stable knowledge of the virtue or vice particular to some bodily action. Virtue is a steady habit, not an occasional act. Interpreters who object to this demand are applying an epistemology that is simply foreign to Plato.

In view of *Euthyphro*, Aristotle's understanding of Platonic epistemology must in some respects be doubted. He certainly had an outward awareness of Plato's arguments, but there is no evidence that he appreciated the grammatical foundation of Plato's metaphysics of Ideas. Aristotle seems to have been more interested in developing his own philosophical positions in a dialectic with Plato's than in understanding his onetime instructor's doctrine from within. Plato and Aristotle were proceeding from fundamentally different intuitions.

Plato's Ideas are clearly separate from the bodily instances that participate in them, but do the Ideas have intelligible relations amongst themselves like those that material bodies possess, or do they stand in isolation? For Plato they do in fact possess relationships analogous to those observed in bodies. It is Parmenides again who argues thus:

"Because, Socrates, I think that you or another, anyone in fact who proposes that there exists in itself some essence of each thing, will agree first of all that not one of them exists in us." "Indeed, for how then would it exist in and of itself?" replied Socrates. "Beautifully spoken," he said. "Then as many of the Ideas as exist in relation to each other have their essence in relation to themselves, but not in relation to their likenesses, or whatever they are called, and are participated by us, from which we are assigned names. And these bodily things, which bear for us the same names, are again in relation to themselves, but not in relation to the Ideas, and belong to themselves, but do not belong to the Ideas that are also named in this way." "How do you mean?" said Socrates. "I mean," replied Parmenides, "just such a thing: If one of us is the master or slave of anyone, he surely is not the slave of master-in-itself, that is, of what a master is, or the master of slave-in-itself, that is, of what a slave is. To the contrary, being a man, both things belong to a man, while mastery itself is of slavery itself, and in the same manner slavery itself is to mastery itself, but things in us do not have their power in relation to the Ideas, nor do the Ideas in relation to us. Rather, I say, the Ideas belong to themselves and are in relation to themselves and, in the same manner, our things are in relation to themselves." (*Parmenides* 133c-134a)

The realm of Ideas exists parallel to that of the corporeal world, but the Idea is one and its participated instances many. Consequently, although the Ideas have relationships amongst themselves, they differ in being relations in the abstract, just as the terms of those relations are abstract, whereas bodies, being multiple, have relationships only with other individual bodies, not with body in the abstract or even with all bodies taken together.

To return now to the original question, were holiness bodily, as Euthyphro and, by extension, Meletus seem to understand it, then it would have merely the capacity for action or passion. It could be acted upon by one body, perhaps, and in turn act upon another. Thus, it would certainly be true that "Not *because it is a thing being loved is it loved* by those by whom it is loved, but *because it is loved it is a thing being loved.*" However, of the Idea one may also assert, "*Because it is a thing causing to be loved it is loved* by those by whom it is loved, but not *because it is loved is it a thing causing to be loved.*" Euthyphro's agreement with Socrates' proposition is only correct of bodies understood as agents and patients. Because he has not turned his mind to the Ideas, he cannot see that the proposition runs contrariwise if it is no longer a thing being loved, but a thing causing to be loved.

The contradiction, therefore, disappears when the Holy is understood as an Idea, rather than a body or an attribute of a body. Leaving to the side the question of whether being loved by the gods is an adequate definition of the Holy, once the Idea is distinguished properly from its participating instances, it does satisfy the requirement of being loved by the gods. That is to say, the following statements are now precise parallels concerning the Holy:

It is loved by the gods because it is *the Holy.*
Not because it is loved by the gods is it *the Holy.*

It is loved by the gods because it is *a thing causing to be loved by the gods.*
Not because it is loved by the gods is it *a thing causing to be loved by the gods.*

One may substitute "a thing causing to be loved by the gods" for "the Holy" without contradiction. The metaphysical status of the Ideas has been decisively established. Participation is not by likeness or any other formal relation. The Idea is distinguished from its bodily instance by one thing only: its transcendent causal power in every order of action and passion.

Euthyphro: But, Socrates, I for my part am unable to say to you what I have in mind. For whatever we propose to ourselves somehow goes about endlessly, not wanting to remain where we seat it.

The line of questioning proceeds to the problem of motion. Euthyphro complains that he is incapable of speaking what he has in mind. The proposals do not want to stay put, but contradictions unseat every assertion. Euthyphro's lament about being unable to keep his explanations from wandering exposes his true problem: He does not possess knowledge but is borne about by unstable opinion. As Socrates observes in his playful etymology:

> From these things, let us first take up this word "knowledge" (ἐπιστήμη) and observe that it is quite double-edged, and it would seem to signify that the soul comes to a standstill upon things, rather than that it is carried around with them. (*Cratylus* 437a)

Socrates: Euthyphro, your arguments would appear to belong to Daedalus, my ancestor. And if I were making them and laying them down, perhaps you would jest with me that on account of my kinship with him my works in words run away and do not wish to remain where one puts them. But now the suppositions are your own; there is need of some other jest. For they do not want to stay put for you, as is apparent even to yourself.

Socrates then jokes with Euthyphro, mentioning that he himself is descended from Daedalus, who was famed for producing mechanical objects that would move about. The claim of descent is not a literal one: according to tradition, the father of Socrates, Sophroniscus, was a sculptor. Through that paternity he could claim in jest to be descended from the ancient Daedalus, who was said to excel all others in these arts. Is then Socrates causing these "works in words" to move about? He denies it, stating flatly that these opinions that cannot withstand criticism belong to Euthyphro himself.

These statues of Daedalus appear elsewhere in Plato's works. A more detailed discussion takes place in *Meno.* The question investigated there is the difference between knowledge and true opinion. It appears that true opinion is no less useful in the practical sphere than is knowledge:

> Socrates: Then true opinion is no worse a leader than understanding with regard to the correctness of action; and this is what we just now left out in our examination concerning virtue, as to what it might be, saying that understanding alone leads to right action, but now there is true opinion.

Meno: It seems so.

Socrates: Then right opinion is no less beneficial than knowledge.

Meno: With this exception, at least, Socrates, that he who has knowledge will always hit the mark, but he who has true opinion will sometimes hit the mark, sometimes not.

Socrates: What do you mean? Will he who has true opinions not always hit the mark, so long as he opines correctly?

Meno: It seems to me a necessity, and so I wonder, Socrates, this being so, that knowledge should ever be so much more honored than right opinion, and what makes the former one thing and the latter another. (*Meno* 97b-d)

So long as an opinion is true, there will be no difference in the practical sphere between action based upon opinion and upon knowledge. Meno is at a loss as to why one should then esteem knowledge so highly. It is here that Socrates introduces the "glorious statues of Daedalus" to provide an answer to Meno's perplexity:

Socrates: Do you know then what makes you wonder, or shall I tell you?

Meno: Tell me, certainly.

Socrates: It is because you have not turned your mind toward the glorious statues of Daedalus. But perhaps there are none among your people.

Meno: To what end do you say this?

Socrates: That these also, if not bound, escape and run away, but, if bound, they stay at hand.

Meno: What of that?

Socrates: If you acquire one of his works that has been set free, it is of little value, like a runaway slave; it will not stay with you; but when bound, it is worth a great deal; for these works are very beautiful. But then, with regard to what am I saying these things? With regard to true opinions. For true opinions, as long as they stay put, are a beautiful possession and work all noble things. However, they do not wish to stay with us very long, but flee from the human soul, so that they are not worth much until they are bound by causes in rational argument. This, Meno, my dear comrade, is recollection, as we agreed previously. But when they are bound, they first turn into knowledge, and then become steadfast. And it is on account of these things that knowledge is more valuable than true opinion: knowledge differs from true opinion by the bond. (*Meno* 97d-98a)

Daedalus was said to be a sculptor and artisan of such skill that his statues were able to move about. These "glorious statues of Daedalus" are valuable when they are in hand, but they tend to wander away, just as the opinions of Euthyphro do. To be of permanent value they must be bound by reason to their cause. The traditional definition of science (ἐπιστήμη) is thus "knowledge through causes." At this point, true opinion becomes "a beautiful possession," that is, a work in conformity with the Idea, as explained already. The process of attaining knowledge consists therefore in binding the opinion. And one may already surmise that this bond is the causal character of the Idea, expressed in the middle voice as "to cause to be known." It is in elevating the mind to embrace the Idea itself that knowledge is produced out of true opinion, and this coincides with opinion remaining beautiful, that is, conformed to the divine Idea. In a statement unusual for its simplicity and directness, Socrates affirms, "knowledge differs from true opinion by the bond."

In retrospect, Euthyphro's description of his father's actions takes on a completely different character. It has been shown already that farming is a metaphor for education. Socrates, as spiritual father to Meletus, was prosecuted for teaching and, in particular, for teaching one of those who was either a sophist or worked alongside the sophists. Socrates bound the "hireling," who was wandering about like a drunken man in his unstable opinions, with the bond of knowledge, leading to the man's death, that is, to his emancipation from the bodily and changeable. The man died from the cold and his bonds, mirroring the death of Socrates himself in *Phaedo*:

> And he who had administered the drug, after binding him and waiting a time, examined his feet and legs, and then, having pressed his feet hard, asked him if he sensed it. Socrates said, "no." And after that in turn the thighs, and ascending in this way, the man showed that Socrates was growing cold and becoming stiff. (*Phaedo* 117e-118a)

Socrates, having spent his life practicing death (*Phaedo* 64a), finally attained the sort of death he sought. The gradual loss of feeling in his legs signifies the passage from sensation to intellectual understanding. It should be noted that ψύχοιτό, which is rendered here as "was growing cold," is related to the Greek ψυχή, or "soul." Socrates is leaving the arena of bodies and entering the realm of soul. Moreover, πηγνῦτο, which has been rendered "was becoming stiff," is connected to the process of fixing plants, or planting, again a figure of education. Thus, the work of instruction carried out by Socrates is no crime, but wholly praiseworthy. Meletus has brought forth an unholy indictment against Socrates, prosecuting him for the latter's teaching, just as Euthyphro has brought an indictment against his father for binding the drunken hireling.

Self-Motion and Soul

Euthyphro: But it seems to me that these definitions call for the joke well enough, Socrates, for I am not the one who has put into them this going about and not remaining, but you seem to me to be the Daedalus, since from my part these things would be staying put.

Socrates: Then, my companion, I have perhaps become more adept in the art than even that great man, inasmuch as he was making only his own works to not remain, but I both my own works, so it would seem, and those of another...

Here begins a debate to determine which of the two is the genuine Daedalus and, by extension, who, in this dialogue of fathers and sons, is Icarus, the son of Daedalus. The question is linked to that of self-motion and the soul. It is clear enough that the proposals of Socrates are taken up by Euthyphro as his own. In that sense Euthyphro is clearly the Daedalus responsible for them, and they certainly do not stay put. Socrates would then be the Icarus who, with Euthyphro's simulacra of genuine wings, attempts to follow him.

But is not Socrates at some level setting these statements in motion by his questioning? If so, then he is indeed doing more than Daedalus, for, as he says, he is not only setting his own works into motion, but the works of another, namely Euthyphro's. Here arises the problem of the origin of motion, which, in Plato's cosmos, is the problem of the soul. In *Phaedrus*, Socrates engages in a lengthy discourse on the nature of soul, which is identified with self-motion:

> Every soul is immortal. For that which is ever moving is immortal, but that which moves another or is moved by another, when it has a cessation of motion has also a cessation of life. Only that which moves itself, since it does not depart from itself, never leaves off moving, and this is the source and fount of motion for as many things as are moved. But the beginning is ungenerated. For it is necessary that everything that is generated be generated from a source, but the source never so. For if the source were to be generated from something, it would not be generated from the source. And since it is ungenerated, it is necessarily incorruptible. With the source destroyed, it would be unable to be generated from something else, nor will another be generated from it, since it is necessary that all things be generated from a beginning. Thus, the source of motion is that which moves itself, and this is unable to be destroyed or generated. Otherwise, the whole of heaven and all generation, failing, will be made to stand still and will never again be set in motion. But since that which is moved by itself has been revealed to be immortal, someone who says that self-motion is the very definition and essence of soul will not be disgraced. For every body that has its motion from without is soulless, but that which has it from within itself, is ensouled, this being the very nature of soul. But if this is so, that the thing that moves itself is nothing other than the soul, then out of necessity the soul would be ungenerated and immortal. (*Phaedrus* 245c-246a)

One must immediately foreclose any misinterpretation that would result from the translation of Platonic motion into Aristotelian terms. Aristotle famously defined motion as "the entelechy of a being in potency in so far as it is in potency." (*Physics* 201b5) "Entelechy" literally means the state of being in its end. A being in motion is not in its end insofar as it is actual, but insofar as it is potential. Aristotle thus distinguishes the motion itself from the final term of motion. The perfect actualization of the being is incompatible with an act of motion, for the former would leave no potency for motion. Consequently, immutability and potentiality are opposed. Moreover, passion in the moved implies action in the mover. The mover moves the moved by imparting act, which the moved receives passively. Clearly, in keeping with Aristotle's metaphysical principles, there must be a first *unmoved mover*, for the first principle of motion cannot include potency, or else it would demand another mover prior to itself. And thus, there is a first mover for every separate motion, a god for each heavenly sphere. (Aristotle, *Metaphysics* 1073a14-15) Aristotle most certainly rejected the notion that the first mover could be a *self-mover*. Yet this is precisely what Plato maintains:

> **Athenian Stranger:** I mean this. Whenever one thing merely impels another, and that in turn another without end, will there ever be some first thing impelling the others? How can that which is moved by another ever be the first of things being altered? It is impossible. But when that which moves itself alters another, and that in turn another, and thousands upon tens of thousands of things are set in motion, can the source of their dependent motions be anything but the impulse of that which has moved itself?

> **Clinias:** Beautifully spoken. One must agree.

> **Athenian Stranger:** Yet let us speak further of this and make answer to ourselves. If all things, uniting as one, were made to stand still, as most men of this sort dare to say, then which among those previously mentioned motions would necessarily come to be first? Surely that which moves itself; for it cannot receive an antecedent impetus from others when there is no antecedent impetus in them. Now, since the origin of all motions and the first that comes to be in both things at rest and things set in motion is the self-moving, we shall say that it is necessarily the most ancient and powerful principle of all, but that whatever is altered by another and in turn moves others is secondary. (*Laws* 894e-895b)

Note that Plato posits that self-motion can arise from rest: "the origin of all motions and the first that comes to be in both things at rest and things set in motion is the self-moving." Plato's conception of motion (κίνησις) is wider in logical extension than that of Aristotle. Wherever there is a junction of action and passion, there is motion. For instance, sensation, which takes place through bodies, is a motion, for it involves both an action (sensing) and a passion (being sensed). Knowledge too is a form of motion in Plato, for there is a knowing, a being known, and ultimately a causing-to-be-known, whether the third principle belongs to thing known, as in knowledge of an Idea, or is supplied externally by the Idea, as in the knowledge of a body. Eternal and changeless knowledge of an Idea is still motion, because it includes action and passion. Whereas Aristotle conceives motion as the act that carries an initial term into the final term of motion, Plato conceives motion as a state, without regard to terms of motion. This state of motion has a priority over any actual change that may occur. When he wishes to imply change, he adds other terms to clarify.

Recall the war between the gods and giants about what is real. Certainly, Plato favors the Olympian gods and the heavenly, but one may be surprised to find that he is in some respects acting as a mediator between the two warring camps. Theaetetus is asked in *Sophist* to answer to the Stranger not only for the earthborn, but for these "friends of Ideas":

> **Stranger:** Then let us go to the others, the friends of Ideas. And please interpret for us their doctrines.

> **Theaetetus:** I will do that.

Stranger: Tell me, do you distinguish between generation and essence? Is it so?

Theaetetus: Yes.

Stranger: And you say that by the body through sensation we share in generation, but that by the soul through reckoning we share in real essence, which you affirm ever maintains itself the same, whereas generation differs from one time to another.

Theaetetus: We do say that. (*Sophist*, 248a-b)

"Friends of Ideas" are those who distinguish between two orders, the order of the generated and ever-changing, and the order of the immutable essences. It is with the aid of the body that the soul senses, whereas essences are perceived by the soul alone, without aid of bodily organ.

Stranger: But, you excellent man, how shall we define this sharing that you say is in both? Is it not what we just now mentioned?

Theaetetus: What sort of thing?

Stranger: A suffering or making that is generated by some power of things being joined to each other.

Theaetetus: What is it they say then?

Stranger: They do not concede to us what we said just now to the earthborn about essence.

Theaetetus: What sort of thing?

Stranger: We set up as a sufficient definition of beings: whenever a power to suffer or do is present in even the least degree.

Theaetetus: Yes.

Stranger: With regard to these things, they say that generation shares in the power to suffer and do, but neither power is joined with being. (*Sophist*, 248b-c)

Recall that Plato defines "being" as that which possesses the "power to suffer or do." That is, being is whatever can act or be acted upon. This is precisely what is shared by body and essence: "A suffering or making that is generated by some power of things being joined to each other." As stated before, soul exceeds body by virtue of its causing-to-be-acted-upon but has in common with body its acting and being acted upon. The "friends of Ideas" apparently do not share in this conception. They maintain that suffering and doing are attributes of generation but are unconnected to the question of being. Presumably, several followers of Socrates had taken up the question of the status of the Ideas and had restricted action and passion to the world of becoming and generation. Since they posit no ontological foundation for participation, it is likely that these same individuals maintained the doctrine of participation by similitude. Plato, through the Stranger, must give answer to their conception of reality:

Theaetetus: Is there something in what they say?

Stranger: We must reply that we need to learn from them more clearly if they concede that the soul knows and that essence is known.

Theaetetus: They do in fact say this.

Stranger: Well then, do they say that knowing or being known is an action or passion or both? Or that the one is a passion and the other is an action? Or that neither of these in any way partakes of these things?

Theaetetus: Clearly, neither would partake in either, for otherwise they would be speaking these things in contradiction. (*Sophist*, 248c-d)

If the "friends of Ideas" do in fact know essences, and the essences are consequently known by the "friends of Ideas," then it follows from their own principles that neither knowing nor being known could be an action or passion.

Stranger: I take your meaning. This at least: If to know is in fact to do something, it necessarily follows that the thing being known suffers something. Now essence, according to this argument, since it is known by the mind, is also on account of this suffering moved to the same extent that it is known, which, we say, does not happen with rest.

Theaetetus: That is right.

Stranger: By the gods, then what? Really, will we be easily persuaded that motion and life and soul and understanding are completely lacking to being, that it neither lives nor understands, but august and holy, lacking mind, is fixed and without motion? (*Sophist* 248d-249a)

According to the "friends of Ideas" then, true being or essence would lack all motion, life, soul, and understanding. Plato, unlike Aristotle, adheres strictly to grammatical usage as the touchstone of metaphysics. If grammatical distinctions are founded upon reality, then one must admit that there is action and passion in the Ideas themselves. Only then will they possess the divine attributes of life and knowledge. Moreover, if the "friends of Ideas" are correct, not only will the gods lack these attributes, but man as well:

Stranger: It must be conceded that motion and the thing being set in motion are as beings.

Theaetetus: How could it be otherwise?

Stranger: Then it is established, Theaetetus, that if beings are unmoved, then there is no mind concerning anything in anyone anywhere. (*Sophist* 249b)

If beings are unmoved, then there is no action and passion, and if no action and passion, then no knowing and being known. If there is to be knowledge, then there can be nothing unmoved, taken in the sense in which Plato understands motion. Thus, there can be no unmoved mover, only a self-moved mover, and this is what Plato understands to be the nature of soul. Aristotle, for his part, deviates from grammatical usage. For Aristotle, seeing, though expressed in the active voice, is in fact a passive process: The object acts upon the senses, which are completely passive. Moreover, for Aristotle the intellect is active in the process of abstraction, but the abstracted species by which one knows is received passively by the intellect.

Soul the First Mover

How does one recognize soul working in the world? One must look for this characteristic of self-motion. Body can be moved and in turn move another. That which can move both itself and another possesses soul:

> **Athenian Stranger:** If we were to see this motion coming to be in something earthy, watery, or fiery, either separately or in a mixture, what state should we say belongs to such a thing?
>
> **Clinias:** You are not asking whether we should address something as "alive" when it moves itself by itself, are you?
>
> **Athenian Stranger:** Yes.
>
> **Clinias:** Alive? Well, how could it not be?
>
> **Athenian Stranger:** Well, then whenever we see soul in things, it's not otherwise, is it? Must we not agree that they are also alive?
>
> **Clinias:** It is just as you say.
>
> **Athenian Stranger:** Now hold on, by Zeus! Would you wish to know three things about each? (*Laws* 895c)

The Athenian Stranger in Plato's *Laws* points out that whenever one sees something moving itself, one recognizes it as living. Fittingly, he proceeds to invoke Zeus, of whom Socrates says in *Cratylus*:

> For there is no one at all, other than the ruler and king of all, who is the cause of life (ζῆν) for us and for all others. Therefore, this god happens to be named rightly, through whom (δι' ὃν) life (ζῆν) begins for all things that live. (*Cratylus* 395e-396b)

The Athenian Stranger then gives a strict definition of "soul" as "the motion with power to move itself":

> **Clinias:** What do you mean by that?
>
> **Athenian Stranger:** One is the essence, one is the definition of the essence, and one is the name. Additionally, there are two things that must be asked about everything that exists.
>
> **Clinias:** How two?
>
> **Athenian Stranger:** At one time a person stretching out the name demands in return the definition; at another time, stretching out the definition, he demands in return the name.
>
> **Clinias:** Do we wish to say something of that sort again now?
>
> **Athenian Stranger:** What sort of thing?
>
> **Clinias:** There is, I suppose, something divisible into halves, both in number and other things. In respect to number its name is "the even," the definition being "number that is divisible into two equal parts."

Athenian Stranger: Yes. I'm showing just such a thing. So, is it not the same thing in each case that we are addressing, whether being asked the definition we return the name, or being asked the name we return the definition, addressing the same being by the name "even" and by the definition "a number divisible into halves"?

Clinias: Altogether so.

Athenian Stranger: And the thing named "soul", what is its definition? Do we have any other than that already pronounced, "the motion with power to move itself"? (*Laws* 895d-896a)

Plato prefaces the definition of soul ("the motion with power to move itself") with an example of definition taken from the odd and even. In discussing the disagreements and enmities of the gods and giants the odd and even were used as an example about which one may suitably come to a peaceable resolution by rational means. In the *Laws*, Plato uses this to establish a Pythagorean metaphorical connection between "even" and "body," on account of the divisibility of body, and by implication "odd" and "soul." We are to understand that this argument about body and soul is precisely what divides the "gods" and "giants," or rather, the spiritual and materialist thinkers. This reference to odd and even will appear later in *Euthyphro*. Note that it is the character of a definition that its converse be true. If something is "soul," then it is a "motion with power to move itself," and if something is a "motion with power to move itself," then it is "soul."

The Athenian Stranger proceeds to argue that motion must be initiated by a self-mover:

Clinias: So, you are saying that the definition "self-motion" and the name "soul" refer altogether to the same essence?

Athenian Stranger: I do say so. And if the matter stands thus, do we still worry that it has not been sufficiently demonstrated that soul is itself the first beginning and motion of what is, what has been, and what will come to be–and of all their contraries–since it is the cause in all respects of impulse and the whole of motion?

Clinias: Not at all. It has been shown most adequately that the soul is the most ancient of all things, being the principle of motion itself.

Athenian Stranger: And the motion that comes to be in one thing through another, but which itself never furnishes causing-to-be-moved to another, is it not second, or as far down the sequence of numbers as you might wish to count, since it is just the impulse of a body without soul?

Clinias: Rightly said.

Athenian Stranger: Then we would have spoken rightly and authoritatively things most true and complete to say that soul has come to be before the body, but the body after, and that the body is governed according to nature by the governing soul.

Clinias: Things most true, indeed. (*Laws* 896a-c)

Body can move another and itself be moved, but it "never furnishes causing-to-be-moved to another." Only soul is capable of initiating motion, for it not only moves and is moved, but causes to be moved, both itself and others. It has the character of not only the active and passive voices, but the middle voice as well. Thus, every chain of bodies in motion, each providing impulse to the next, must be traced back to the first mover, which is always ensouled, that is, self-moving.

After this long digression, it is now possible to interpret the observation of Socrates: *"I have perhaps become more adept in the art than even that great man, inasmuch as he was making only his own works to not remain, but I both my own works, so it would seem, and those of another."* Socrates, playing the part of soul, is conferring the "causing-to-be-moved" to Euthyphro's arguments. As the self-moved mover, he does not allow them to remain where they are put but sets all in motion. He transcends the merely bodily causation of impulse, that of Euthyphro, who is the true Daedalus.

Body and Soul

Another digression, once again into *Cratylus*, will help one to understand the relationship between body and soul:

> **Socrates:** I think that ["body" (σῶμα)] can be explained in numerous ways, if it is bent but a little, even a very little; for some say that it is the tomb (σῆμα) of the soul, which has been buried during the present life, and, moreover, because through the body the soul signifies (σημαίνει) the things it signifies, for this is it rightly called a "sign" (σῆμα). But the Orphic poets appear to have given this name primarily because the soul has been given a punishment for something. They say that the soul is encompassed by the body in order that the soul may be made secure (σῴζηται), which is a likeness of prison. And the body is, as it is thus named, the "secure place" (σῶμα) of the soul, until it pays off what is owed, and then one does not even need to change a letter. (*Cratylus* 440b-c)

In the hermeneutic key of the *Cratylus*, Socrates seeks to derive the meaning of body (σῶμα) from similar word forms. Inverting the common notion of life and death, the body is the tomb (σῆμα) of the soul, because the soul rests in it during this life. It is also a sign, for it is through the body that the soul signifies. Finally, it is the "secure place" (σῶμα) or prison of the soul. In this reading one should call to mind Plato's famed "Allegory of the Cave" (*Republic* 514a-520a). By his reckoning, turning toward bodies is a positive hindrance to genuine knowledge of essences. On the other hand, soul is the principle of life:

> **Socrates:** To speak on the spot, I think that those who gave a name to the soul had in mind some such thing: that when it was present to the body, it was the cause of its living, by reviving (ἀναψῦχον) the body and furnishing it with the power to breathe. But when this vivifying power quits the body, the body perishes and comes to an end, wherefore these

appear to me have called it "soul" (ψυχή). But if you wish, hold on a minute. I think I
have in view something more persuasive than this for the followers of Euthyphro. For I
think they would despise it and would consider it vulgar. Now see if this will make amends
to you.

Hermogenes: Just say it. (*Cratylus* 399d-400a)

It is the soul (ψυχή) that possesses life of itself and confers it upon body by its union with it,
thus reviving (ἀναψῦχον) it. Yet Socrates points out that this meaning will be unsatisfactory
to Euthyphro and his followers. For their sake, he begins a second derivation:

Socrates: Does it seem to you that there is anything, other than the soul, that holds and bears
the nature of the entire body, with the result that it both lives and moves about?

Hermogenes: Nothing else.

Socrates: Well, then do you not believe Anaxagoras that it is mind and soul which regulate
and hold the nature of all other things?

Hermogenes: I do.

Socrates: Then it would be beautiful to assign the name "nature-holder" (φυσέχην) to the
power that bears and holds (ἔχει) nature (φύσιν), and call it, once refined, "soul" (ψυχή).

Hermogenes: Certainly, then. And it appears to me that this latter explanation is done more
artfully than the former.

Socrates: And indeed it is. But it seems ridiculous that the name was truly assigned this way.
(*Cratylus* 400a-b)

An alternative explanation of soul is that it holds (ἔχει) the nature (φύσιν) of the entire
body, for which reason "soul" derives from "nature-holder" (φυσέχην). This explanation
is more in keeping with the Aristotelian definition of the soul as the essential or substantial
form of an organic body. There were clearly two competing schools of thought during
Plato's lifetime. However, he does not outright reject the theory of Euthyphro about the
nature of the soul. Plato appears to accept that in its union with the body the soul bears
the nature of the body taken as a whole, be that human, simian, or canine. Plato simply
assigns a higher value to the prior explanation, for he considers the soul's separation from
the body as the more perfect form of life:

Socrates: But when the soul observes by itself and in accordance with itself, it goes thither
to the pure, the everlasting, the immortal, and the immutable; being kindred to it, the
soul is always assimilated, whenever, permitting itself, it comes to be by itself. The soul's
wandering comes to an end; concerning those things and in conformity with them, it
remains stable, since it is made fast by such things. This condition of the soul is called
understanding. (*Phaedo* 79c-d)

In its communion with the Ideas through understanding, the soul becomes stable and
changeless, like the Ideas themselves. On the other hand, as observed by the Stranger in
Statesman, attachment to bodies drags the soul back and forth:

<blockquote>

Stranger: To abide always in the same way and to be ever changeless belongs alone to the most divine things of all, and the nature of body is not of this order. (*Statesman* 269d)

</blockquote>

This detachment from bodies and turning toward the changeless and divine is a moral imperative that determines one's destiny, either a descent further into corporality and vice, or an ascent into virtue and holiness:

<blockquote>

Athenian Stranger: Then as many things as partake of soul also change, possessing within themselves the principle of change, and in changing are carried in accordance with the law and order of their particular lot. The smaller the change of character, the less they seek after earthy places, but when they move toward greater injustice, they fall into the depths, into the infernal places, as they are called under a number of names, Hades and the like, of which people are quite terrified, being haunted in dreams both while living and after separated from their bodies. Whenever a soul, on account of its own intention and strong companionship, obtains a greater share of evil or virtue, if it communes with divine virtue, it too becomes preeminently divine, changes onto a holy road, and is transported to a better and more eminent place; but if the opposite, it migrates to the opposite place of life. (*Laws* 904c-e)

</blockquote>

And so it is that the body must always be subject to the soul as the inferior to the superior:

<blockquote>

Although we have put our hand to describing the soul only now, after the body, God did not in like manner contrive it to be younger. For, in causing them to work together, he did not allow the elder to be ruled by the younger. We, however, partaking of the accidental, also speak by accident. But the soul is prior to and older than the body in both birth and excellence and is the mistress and ruler of the body thus ruled. (*Timaeus* 34b-c)

</blockquote>

The Wealth of Tantalus

... What's more, this art of mine is most ingenious because I am wise against my will. For I would have wished my words to stay in place and be made to sit down motionless, more than to obtain the wisdom of Daedalus and the wealth of Tantalus.

Socrates refuses Euthyphro's suggestion in the sense Euthyphro meant it to be understood. He points out that by this reasoning he would be wise against his own will, an impossible conclusion. For it is the foolish who are foolish against their own will on account of their lack of knowledge. Socrates would have his works in words to remain where he has seated them, and he desires this more than the "wisdom of Daedalus and the wealth of Tantalus." The "wisdom of Daedalus" is clearly a fake wisdom, indeed a form of foolishness.

One must call to mind the myth of Daedalus and Icarus, his son, a myth that lends additional structure to the dialogue. The "wings" of Daedalus are merely mechanical imitations. When Icarus attempts to fly too high, the wax melts and they fail to function, leading to his death. Daedalus is indeed a poor father to his son.

But what of the "wealth of Tantalus"? Tantalus was proverbially wealthy, and so at the superficial level one may understand that Socrates values knowledge over any quantity of physical riches. This statement is, however, a much more pointed remark about one of the contemporaries of Socrates. In *Protagoras*, Socrates describes his visit to the home of Callias, where Protagoras and several other sophists have congregated. Quoting Homer's *Odyssey*, Socrates affirms, "Yes, 'and I saw Tantalus,' for Prodicus of Ceos was in the city." (*Protagoras* 315c) Such an identification is no passing joke but yet another key to unlocking the meaning of the present dialogue. The reference, which would have been clear to any Athenian with a basic literary familiarity, is to the descent of Odysseus into the underworld:

> Aye, and I saw Tantalus in violent torment, standing in a pool, and the water came nigh unto his chin. He seemed as one athirst, but could not take and drink; for as often as that old man stooped down, eager to drink, so often would the water be swallowed up and vanish away, and at his feet the black earth would appear, for some god made all dry. And trees, high and leafy, let stream their fruits above his head, pears, and pomegranates, and apple trees with their bright fruit, and sweet figs, and luxuriant olives. But as often as that old man would reach out toward these, to clutch them with his hands, the wind would toss them to the shadowy clouds. (*Odyssey* 11.582-592)

The true wealth of Tantalus consists in forever being unable to grasp any fruit by his hand or bring water to his mouth. Eternally thirsting and starving, he is unable to satisfy his desire. In *Protagoras* 339e-341e, Socrates refers to Prodicus a question about the meaning of the word "awful," for the latter claimed a special ability to distinguish meanings, but instead Prodicus gets everything wrong and is made to appear ridiculous in his pretentions. One may add to this the playful, yet grievous, derivation of his name: Socrates derives "Tantalus" (Τάνταλος) from "most wretched" (ταλάντατον). (*Cratylus* 395e) This is the condemnation made of Prodicus of Ceos. Prodicus was one of a handful of sophists who made enormous quantities of money by going about the Greek cities, persuading young men to pay him for lessons. He was considered an atheist. We have from Sextus Empiricus:

> But Prodicus said that what is of benefit to life was raised to the level of a god, such as the sun, moon, rivers, lakes, grassy meadows, crops and everything of that sort.
>
> Against the Physicists (Mathematicians) I.52

The gods then were merely assignations made by men to whatever was a benefit to human life. (Note the later discussion about "the beneficial.") The notion of Prodicus was clearly that there is no genuinely divine element in the cosmos, and that man ought to live according to naturalistic, and presumably materialistic, principles.

One finds also in *Cratylus* 384b a reference in which Socrates bewails his inability to explain the origin of names because he has only taken the one-drachma course of Prodicus, instead of the fifty-drachma course. The source of this "wealth of Tantalus" is therefore no mystery. Euthyphro, whom Socrates named in *Cratylus* as being inspired in this matter, likely learned his art from Prodicus, and if the identity of Euthyphro with Meletus is accepted, Meletus himself was taught by Prodicus the art of wordsmithing. Indeed, Meletus accused Socrates on behalf of the poets. This would certainly give a very hypocritical and cynical turn to the accusations of Meletus that Socrates did not acknowledge the gods of the state.

> *But enough of these things! Since you seem to me to fare languidly and sumptuously, I myself will be zealous in your behalf, that you may teach me about the holy.*

After alluding to Tantalus and his wealth, the claim of Socrates that Euthyphro is one who seems "to fare languidly and sumptuously" is particularly arresting. The most horrific crime of Tantalus was to have convoked a great feast for the gods, serving up his own son as one of the courses. In this dialogue, Euthyphro assumes fatherhood to himself, a complete inversion of the reality of things. Euthyphro, and by extension Meletus, is showing himself to be a father not unlike Tantalus.

Generation According to the Earthborn

For there to be generation and change, there must, according to Plato, be three classes of things. The first class is that of the Ideas: changeless, eternal, communicated by teaching, and contemplated intellectually only by the gods and a small group of men, the genuine philosophers. The second class is that of bodies: generated, ever-changing, apprehended by mere opinion, and perceived by all men. The third is "ever existing place," the receptacle of all that is generated:

> If mind and opinion are truly two distinct classes, then these ideas, existing in and by themselves, imperceptible to the senses but seen by the mind, undoubtedly exist. However, if, as it appears to some, opinion truly differs in nothing from mind, then all things, as many as are perceived through the body, are to be reckoned most stable. Now these two must be spoken of severally, because they came into being separately, being unlike each other. For the one comes to be in us through teaching, but the other through persuasion. The one is always in the company of true reason, but the other is without reason. And whereas the one cannot be moved by persuasion the other is easily swayed. Finally, it must be said that all men partake of the latter, but only the gods and a small class of men partake of the former.

With matters standing thus, it must be agreed that one class is the Idea in and by itself, not generated but indestructible, neither taking to itself any other thing from any other place, nor itself going anywhere into another. Being invisible and otherwise insensible, it is the mind's portion to examine it. The second is like-named and similar to it, but grasped by the senses, generated, always being moved to-and-fro, coming to be in some place and being destroyed out of it, apprehended by opinion joined to sensation. And yet again a third class is ever existing place, not admitting of destruction and furnishing a place in which may be seated as many things as have generation, itself being touched upon without the senses by a certain bastard calculation, scarcely something to be believed. (*Timaeus* 51d-52b)

The third, this receptacle, is understood only "by a certain bastard calculation." The choice of words is not accidental, for Plato presents generation in the manner of a family, with the ensouled Idea represented by the father, the generated as the offspring of the father, and that which receives it as the mother:

For the present then it is necessary to keep in our mind three classes: the thing being generated, that in which it is generated, and that from which the thing being generated is copied and engendered. It is fitting, moreover, that the thing receiving be imagined as the mother, the thing from which it is copied as the father, and the nature begotten in their midst as the offspring. One must also realize that if the imprinted thing is destined to change to tapestries of every embroidered color, then that in which the imprinted thing is placed would not be well prepared to receive it unless it were altogether without the form of those Ideas which it might be destined to receive from elsewhere. (*Timaeus* 50c-d)

The receptacle itself cannot be generated, for there would be nothing in which to generate it. There also cannot be an eternal Idea, a genuine father, of the receptacle. Consequently, its origin must be reckoned as something outside of legitimate begetting. It is a "bastard calculation." Consider once again the reference to many-colored tapestries, here to point out the variability and change that is inherent to the generated order, like the topsy-turvy motions of a democratic polity.

Those who deny the Ideas as the causes of all generation necessarily repeat the crime of Oedipus. The father, here in the role of Idea, is murdered, and the son, as the current occupant of the receptacle, begets a new occupant. This process is continued *ad infinitum*. The previously mentioned but obscure advice of the Stranger to Theaetetus on combatting materialist doctrines now makes far more sense:

Accordingly, they who argue against them defend themselves very piously with the unseen from above, contending that true being and essence consists in intelligible but bodiless ideas. But the bodies of those other men and their so-called truth they will break down into tiny pieces in their arguments, addressing them not as essence, but as a certain generation being carried along. (*Sophist*, 246c)

This "certain generation being carried along" is an Oedipal conception of change in which one body incestuously generates the next. Of this one may repeat from *Oedipus the King* concerning the begetter:

Antistrophe: Time who sees all has found you out
against your will; judges your marriage accursed,
begetter and begot at one in it.
(*Oedipus the King*, 1213-1215)

And of the receptacle one may say:

2nd Messenger: And then she groaned and cursed the bed in which
she brought forth husband by husband, children
by her own child, an infamous double bond.
(*Oedipus the King*, 1249-1251)

Fear and Reverence

Socrates: And do not give up too soon. For see if it does not seem necessary to you that everything holy is just.

Euthyphro: It does.

Socrates: Is then every just thing also holy, or every holy thing also just, or is not every just thing holy, but some part of the just holy and part of it something else?

Euthyphro: Socrates, I cannot follow your arguments.

Socrates: And yet you are younger than I by as much as you are the wiser. But, as I say, you fare luxuriantly because of your wealth of wisdom. But, blessed man, strain yourself. For to apprehend what I am saying is not difficult. For I am saying the reverse of what the poet said, he who wrote: "But Zeus, who performed these works, planting all these things, do not crave to name. For where there is fear, there also is reverence." Now I differ with this poet. Shall I tell you in what way.

Euthyphro: Certainly.

Socrates now leads Euthyphro to begin his fourth attempt at defining holiness. He starts by proposing that the holy is also just. However, the question remains whether holiness is coextensive with justice or just a part of it. This can be discerned by asking whether there are just things that are not simultaneously holy. If so, then justice is more extensive than holiness and the Holy is simply a part of the Just. Euthyphro does not understand, and Socrates subtly mocks him by creating an inverted analogy: Euthyphro is wiser than Socrates to the degree that he is younger. Euthyphro is less aged, implying that he is also less wise.

Socrates then urges Euthyphro to strain himself once again, using the same language that one would use in stringing a bow. He commences the new line of inquiry by considering the words of a poet. Zeus, the god of friendship and life, is engaged in "planting all these things." In the context of the earlier agricultural metaphor, Plato is evoking the act of teaching. In the poet's opinion, one ought not to give a name to Zeus. The poet reasons, *"Where there is fear, there also is reverence."* Yet Socrates names Zeus explicitly, as seen already in the excerpt from *Cratylus*, a dialogue on the correctness of names. Socrates believes that the poet is in error.

Socrates: *It does not seem to me that where there is fear there is also reverence. For many men fearful of diseases and poverty and many other such things seem to me to fear, but do not revere in any way these things which they fear. Does it not also seem so to you?*

Euthyphro: *Certainly.*

Socrates: *Rather, where there is reverence, there is also fear, for is there anyone who, feeling reverence, is ashamed of some deed, but has not at the same time dreaded or feared the reputation of baseness?*

Euthyphro: *Indeed, he would fear it.*

There are two forms of fear, one connected with the body, the other with the soul. The fears to which the body gives rise are servile in nature: disease and poverty. However, the soul gives rise to a higher form of fear: the fear of the reputation for baseness. Plato takes up this question in the *Laws* as well:

Athenian: So, tell me, are we able to distinguish two nearly opposite ideas of fear?

Clinias: Of what sort?

Athenian: Things of this sort: we are afraid whenever we expect evils.

Clinias: Yes.

Athenian: And often we fear opinion, when we think that we will be reputed evil when doing or saying something unseemly. We, at least, and I think all others, call this fear "shame."

Clinias: Of course.

Athenian: These are the two fears mentioned. The second of these is opposed to pains and to other fears, but also to a multitude of great pleasures. (*Laws* 646e-647a)

This division of fear into what are sometimes called "servile" and "filial" fear, the fear that the slave has of its master's punishments and the fear that a son has of offending his father, has an immediate bearing upon Euthyphro's subsequent claim that holiness consists in a kind of service to the gods. Euthyphro will claim that this service is that which servants render to their masters, whereas it is rather the service that a son renders to his father. Euthyphro's relation to the gods is that of servile fear. And the sum of all such fear is the fear of death: "For to fear death, you men, is nothing but to suppose that one is wise, not being so; for it is to suppose that one knows the things that one does not." (*Apology* 29a)

Socrates: Then it is not right to say, "for where there is fear, there also is reverence," but rather, "where there is reverence, there also is fear." For reverence is not everywhere fear is, since fear, I think, is something larger than reverence. For reverence is but a part of fear, just as the odd is a part of number, with the result that the odd is not everywhere number is, but rather, number is everywhere the odd is. Perhaps you follow now?

Euthyphro: Certainly.

Socrates concludes that reverence and the concomitant fear of baseness is necessarily less extensive than fear in general. Reverence may consequently be considered a part, as it were, of fear, leaving aside the remaining fears, which are servile and corporally motivated. Choosing holiness presupposes an understanding of that in which it consists, which, for Plato, is the cultivation of the soul and its virtues, not of bodily perfections, capacities, or possessions. This choice is decisive for man's salvation:

"Then, if for us acting well consisted in this, in doing and taking things of great length, but not doing and fleeing from small things, what would disclose to us the salvation of our lives? Would it be the art of measurement or the power of appearing? Does not this power cause us to wander and so many times turn things upside down, so that we repent of both our actions and of our choices of the great and slight? On the other hand, the knowledge of measurement would have made this apparition warrantless, and, having shown us the truth, would have brought us to the leisure of resting in that truth, and would thus have preserved our lives. Would people agree, with regard to these things, that it is the art of measurement that saves our lives, or is it something else?" "The metrical art," he agreed. "But what if the salvation of our lives consisted in the choice of odd or even, when one must choose correctly the greater or the lesser number, each in itself and to one another, or whether something is near or far, what would save our lives? Would it not be knowledge? Would it not be the knowledge of measurement, since this art concerns excess and deficiency? And would it be anything other than arithmetic, since it concerns the odd and the even? Would people agree with us or not? (*Protagoras* 356d-357a)

Here the metaphor of odd and even becomes explicit: reverence is to fear as the odd (soul) is to number (soul and body taken together). The nature of holiness, like the odd and even, is a matter upon which the gods, including philosophers, will agree. Differences can be adjudicated in the court of reason.

Socrates: It was such a thing I meant before in asking whether where the just is, the holy is also there, or, where the holy is, there also is the just, but the holy is not everywhere the just is; for the holy is a part of the just. Shall we speak in this way or does it seem otherwise to you.

Euthyphro: No, but in this way. For you seem to me to speak rightly.

Socrates: Now look at what comes next. For if the holy is a part of the just, it is necessary, it would seem, that we find out what sort of part of the just the holy is. If you asked me about some one of the things just discussed, for example, what part of number the even is and what this number happens to be, I would say, "that which has not unequal, but equal divisions." Or does it not seem so to you?

Euthyphro: It does to me.

Socrates returns to the Holy and the Just. He asserts that justice is the more extensive of the two, and holiness a mere part of it, to which Euthyphro gives his assent. But now Socrates demands that Euthyphro explain what part of justice holiness consists in, and he returns to the metaphor of the odd and even. The odd has "unequal" divisions, whereas the even has "equal divisions." In other words, an even number of objects can be divided into two groups of equal number, whereas any division of an odd number of objects must result in two collections differing in number. Inequality and equality, hearkening back again to the odd (soul) and the even (body), become critical to describe the relations of gods and men.

Socrates: Try now to teach me in this way what part of the just the holy is, in order that we may also tell Meletus to no longer wrong us or indict us for impiety, since I have sufficiently learned from you the things that are pious and holy and those that are not.

Euthyphro: It seems to me, Socrates, that the part of the just concerning the tending of the gods is pious and holy, but that the remaining part of the just is that concerning men.

Euthyphro proposes that holiness is that part of justice which concerns the "tending of the gods," whereas that which concerns men pertains to justice, but not holiness.

Socrates: You appear to me to speak beautifully, Euthyphro. But I am still lacking one little thing. For I do not yet understand what sort of thing you call "tending." For you surely do not mean the same sort of tending of the gods as of other things. For we mean, indeed *we affirm, that not everyone knows how to tend horses, but the horse-trainer does. Is it so?*

Euthyphro: Certainly.

Socrates: For I suppose the art of horse training is the tending of horses.

Euthyphro: Yes.

Socrates: Nor does everyone know how to tend dogs, but the hunter does?

Euthyphro: It is so.

Socrates: For I suppose the art of hunting is the tending of dogs.

Euthyphro: Yes.

Socrates: And the art of the oxherd is the tending of oxen?

Euthyphro: Certainly.

Socrates now wishes to understand precisely what sort of tendance is offered to the gods. By way of comparison, he mentions the arts of tending horses, dogs, and oxen. All three of these arts are figures for verbal arts. The art of tending horses signifies the analysis of the origin and meaning of words, the correctness of names, such as may be found in *Cratylus*:

> Socrates: Then, for the sake of the gods, let us leave behind the gods, as I fear to discourse about them, but toss to me whatever others you wish, that you may see what sort of horses Euthyphro has. (*Cratylus* 407d)

The tending of dogs signifies the art of logical division (hunting for definitions) that is used extensively in Plato's *Republic*, in which he criticizes the logic and politics of the Cynics ("guardian-dogs"). The art of the oxherd is that of rhetoric, whereby those without knowledge are guided by persuasion to choose the correct course of action:

> Receiving by allotments of justice that which was dear and then settling these places, they reared us as their own property and nurslings, in the custom of herdsmen. Except, they did not constrain our bodies by bodily means, like a herdsman managing the herd with a stroke of his staff, but guided them aright from the stern, where the animal is most easily turned, by persuasion, as if by a rudder, and in accord with their reason. And in this way did they drive and pilot everything mortal. (*Critias* 109b-c)

There are two ways in which the wingless "bipedal animal" may be herded. The first is that of the tyrant, who uses compulsion to rule over his human flock. The second, the way of the genuine king, is to use the power of persuasion, that the flock may willingly follow his commands. In this sense, to return to an earlier point of the dialogue, the philosopher, who is rightfully called "king" or "statesman," will use the second form of governing, which induces voluntary obedience:

> Stranger: There is one division by which we might have divided the divine shepherd from the human caretaker.
>
> Young Socrates: And quite rightly.

Stranger: But, in turn, it was necessary to cut into two halves the caretaking art thus apportioned.

Young Socrates: By what division?

Stranger: By dividing the enforced from the voluntary.

Young Socrates: Why so?

Stranger: Because, surely, missing the mark before about this, we were more simplistic than we ought to have been when we lumped together the king and the tyrant, whereas both they and the manners of their respective rules are most dissimilar.

Young Socrates: Truly spoken.

Stranger: Then, setting ourselves aright once again, as I just suggested, shall we divide the art of human caretaking into halves by the criterion of enforced and voluntary?

Young Socrates: By all means.

Stranger: And, surely, were we to call the art of raising bipedal animals by force "tyrannical" and the welcome art of raising willing bipedal animals "political," would we not thereby proclaim that he who possesses the latter art of caretaking is really both king and statesman? (*Statesman* 276d-e)

The philosopher-king is the true "divine shepherd" who governs his flock. Note that this "human caretaking" is divided into "halves," indicating by this Pythagorean allusion that this governance of human flocks is merely founded upon correct opinion of the governed. Socrates proceeds to this "tending of the gods," to determine precisely what is meant by it.

Socrates: And the art of holiness and piety is the tending of the gods, Euthyphro? Do you mean this?

Euthyphro: I do.

Socrates: Now does tending always accomplish the same thing? I mean such as this: Is it for the good and benefit of the one being tended, as indeed you see that horses that are tended by the horse trainer are benefited and become better? Do they not seem so to you?

Euthyphro: To me they do.

Socrates: And dogs somehow by the hunter's art and oxen by the oxherd's art, and all other things in the same way? Or do you think that tending is for the harm of the one being tended?

Euthyphro: By Zeus, not I!

Socrates: But for its benefit?

Euthyphro: How otherwise?

Socrates points out that the tendance of anything bodily and perceptible to the senses is meant for its improvement. He then attempts to extend this notion to include the tending of the gods. Would the gods as well benefit and be improved by this care and attention?

Socrates: *Then holiness, being the tending of the gods, is a benefit to the gods and makes the gods better? And would you agree that whenever you do something holy you are making some one of the gods better?*

Euthyphro: *By Zeus, not I!*

Socrates: *Nor, Euthyphro, do I think that you mean this, and far from it! But I was asking for the sake of this, what you might mean by tending of the gods, not in fact thinking that you mean such a thing.*

Euthyphro: *And rightly so, Socrates. For I do not mean such a thing.*

Socrates: *Be it so. But what tending of the gods would holiness be?*

Euthyphro: *That, Socrates, which slaves tend to their masters.*

Once again, Socrates leads Euthyphro down a dead end, if only to understand that it is a dead end, and once again Euthyphro denies that he meant what he had previously said. One should also keep in mind the meaning of "beneficial" as described by Socrates in *Cratylus*:

> "Beneficial" (ὠφέλιμον) is a foreign name, the verbal form of which (ὀφέλλειν) Homer used in many places. It is derived from increasing and making. (*Cratylus* 417c)

"Beneficial" is a foreign name. One ought immediately to think of the foreign sophists, outside of the household of Athens, who traveled there to collect money for their teaching. Indeed, "beneficial" (ὠφέλιμον) "is derived from increasing and making." Understood as a relationship between the sophists and their students, it would imply what will later be called a "mercantile" art between gods and men. However, "increasing and making" can equally be understood of the making of new gods, the teaching of wisdom, in which Socrates was engaged.

In Service of the Gods

Socrates: *I am beginning to understand. It would be, so it would seem, some service to the gods.*

Euthyphro: *Very much so.*

Socrates: *Can you say then, the service to doctors, for the accomplishment of what work is it a service? Do you not think it is for the sake of health?*

Euthyphro: *I do.*

Socrates: *Well, then? The service to shipbuilders, for the accomplishment of what work is it a service?*

Euthyphro: *Clearly, Socrates, for the construction of a ship.*

Socrates: *And the service to builders is for the construction of a house?*

Euthyphro: *Yes.*

Socrates: *Then do tell, best of men, this service to the gods, for the accomplishment of what work would it be a service? For it is clear that you know, since in fact you say that you know about divine things, at least, better than any other man.*

Euthyphro: *And I speak the truth, Socrates.*

Socrates: *Tell me then, in the name of Zeus, whatever could that all-beautiful work be, which the gods accomplish, employing us as servants?*

In serving the doctor, and here we may include the doctor of the soul, one is working toward the goal of health. Likewise, the service to the shipbuilder or builder is the making of a ship or house. What then is the end to which one's services are put in the service of the gods?

Euthyphro: *Many beautiful things, Socrates.*

Socrates: *Yes, and generals too, friend, but you might likewise easily say that the chief of these is that they attain victory in battle. Is it not so?*

Euthyphro: *How otherwise?*

Socrates: *And farmers accomplish many and, I think, beautiful things. But, likewise, the chief of these works is a brood out of the earth.*

Euthyphro: *Certainly.*

In the figure of the soldier and the farmer, Socrates completes his answer: The philosopher serves the gods (Ideas) by warring against the earthborn giants to establish the supremacy of soul, and he does this through the process of teaching.

Prayer and Sacrifice

Socrates: *Well then? Of the many beautiful things that the gods accomplish, what is the chief work?*

Euthyphro: *I told you a little earlier, Socrates, that it is a rather great work to learn accurately how all these things stand. I simply say to you this, that if someone possesses the knowledge of doing and saying things pleasing to the gods by praying and sacrificing, these are holy things, and such things preserve both one's own house and the common interests of cities; but the opposites of these pleasing things are impious, and overturn and destroy everything together.*

Euthyphro, unable to give a satisfactory answer to the promptings of Socrates, reverts to his previous form of answer, neglecting the essence of holiness by simply naming actions that are generally held to be holy. Euthyphro sees only the outward bodily action, completely oblivious to the soul of the one performing the action. Compare the claim of Socrates in the *Republic*:

> I said, "Will you therefore first restore this assertion, namely, that it does not escape the notice of at least the gods what sort of thing each of these two [justice and injustice] is?" "We will restore it," he replied. "But if not unnoticed, the one would be beloved of god and the other hated of god, as we agreed in the beginning." "These things are so." "And shall we not agree that all things, as many as come from the gods, are of the best sort for the one who is beloved of god, unless it is some necessary evil that originated in a former sin?" "Very much so." "Then it must be understood concerning the just man, whether he come into poverty or diseases or any other of the supposed evils, that for him these things will end for the good, both as he lives and dies." (*Republic* 612e-613b)

Even physical evils, "poverty or diseases," these objects of servile fear previously considered, are for the ultimate good of the just man. Holiness and its rewards are not in the material order but are goods of the soul possessed both in the present life and the life thereafter. Man is obliged to turn his soul toward the divine, toward the Ideas, "tending always those things that possess divinity." It is thus that he will partake of the immortal, as is explained in *Timaeus*:

But to him who turns his understanding to the love of learning and truth, hastening to exercise these concerns above his others, to him necessarily does it belong to understand immortal and divine things, which are made fast by truth, and, insofar as human nature is able to partake of immortality, he will then not lack a share of it. Tending always those things that possess divinity and adorning his indwelling spirit, he will be preeminently blessed. And there is but one tendance of each by every other: to render to each the nourishment and motion proper to its household. Congenital to the divine in us are the reasonings and revolutions of the cosmos. It is necessary for each man to accompany these, rectifying the circuits in our head that were corrupted at birth by learning thoroughly the harmonies and revolutions of the cosmos, and, in accord with its original nature, assimilating to the mind what is intuited by the mind, and possessing this likeness as the purpose of the best life, that set forth for men by the gods for both time present and time hereafter. (*Timaeus* 90b-d)

Here Plato sets forth the principle that "there is but one tendance of each by every other: to render to each the nourishment and motion proper to its household." The household of the gods includes the genuine philosophers. Euthyphro's contention that one must prosecute without regard to whether someone is of the same household is thereby rejected. The motion and nourishment proper to the household of the philosophers is that of instruction. Recall that it was in this vein that Socrates had claimed in the *Apology* that if he were guilty of anything, he ought to have been instructed, not punished.

Plato maintains that it is the character of the soul of the one sacrificing that is most important:

For it would be a terrible thing if the gods had regard for our gifts and sacrifices, but not the soul and whether someone happens to be holy and just. (*Alcibiades II* 149e)

The Athenian stranger expands upon this matter in Plato's *Laws*:

What behavior then is beloved of and attendant upon God? One alone, which is contained in the ancient phrase, that like in moderation is beloved of like, but immoderate things are beloved, the one to the other, neither amongst themselves, nor amongst moderate things. And, for us, God is supremely the measure of all things, very much more so than any man, as they claim. The man then who would become endeared to such a God, must, according to his power, become of the same sort. And according to this argument, he amongst us who is temperate is beloved of God, for he is of like character, while he that is intemperate is of unlike character and, being at enmity, is unjust. And the same argument holds in this way with regard to the other virtues. Let us also understand that following those things there is a rule of this sort, of all rules the most beautiful and truthful, that to offer sacrifice to the gods, communicating with them continually by means of prayers and offerings and every manner of service to them, is a thing most beautiful, most noble, and most effectual for a blessed life, and preeminently fitting also, but for the wicked man it brings forth the opposite. For the wicked man is uncleansed in soul, whereas the man of opposite character is cleansed. And no good man or god can ever rightly receive gifts from the defiled. Therefore, the great toil spent upon the gods by the wicked is in vain but is most fruitful to all who are holy. This then is for us the mark at which one must aim. But as regards the arrow, what sort of arrow would be carried most directly to its target? First, we say that if, after distributing honors to the Olympians and to the gods preserving the state, we should distribute to those under the earth the even and the left-handed, we would hit most directly the mark of piety, as we also would in assigning to the Olympians things from above, the odd and honors sounding concordantly with it. (*Laws* 716c-717b)

Plato once again uses the distinction of odd and even (as also of right-handed and left-handed) to distinguish between the realm of soul and body. One must first honor the Olympian gods, the gods of soul and the transcendent, who are accordingly assigned the odd numbers, and only then the gods of the underworld, who are masters of the earth-bound, and therefore assigned the even.

Stringing the Bow

Euthyphro has failed to tell Socrates the chief accomplishment of the tending of the gods. However, Socrates reveals in his response the answer: teaching, that is, the making of new gods. Euthyphro has not only failed to define it, but in the very omission he has also failed to show it by his example: "*If you had answered, I would have already learned from you about holiness.*" One may distinguish in Greek between ἀποδείξις (demonstration by reason) and ἐπιδείξις (demonstration by exhibition). Through the response of Socrates, Plato has united a criticism of Euthyphro embracing both.

Euthyphro has taken on here the persona of Telemachus, son of Odysseus. Prior to the slaying of the suitors, Telemachus tried four times to string the bow of his father:

Then he went and stood upon the threshold and began to try the bow. Thrice he made it quiver in his eagerness to draw it, and thrice he relaxed his effort, though in his heart he hoped to string the bow and shoot an arrow through the iron. And now at the last he would haply have strung it in his might, as for the fourth time he sought to draw up the string, but Odysseus nodded in dissent, and checked him in his eagerness. (*Odyssey* 21.124-130)

Socrates in *Cratylus* links the bow with opinion. Euthyphro, for his part, has already tried three times to define "holiness." First, he claimed that holiness was precisely what he was doing, prosecuting the evildoer, but this turned out to be an example of a holy action, not the Holy in itself. Second, Euthyphro claimed that holiness is whatever is loved by the gods. However, this definition resulted in holiness being both loved and hated by the gods. Third, Euthyphro claimed that holiness is what is loved by all the gods. It was found, however, that holiness is loved by the gods because it is holy. It is not holy because it is loved by the gods. On the other hand, a thing being loved by the gods is such precisely because it is loved by the gods. It is not loved by the gods because it is a thing being loved by the gods.

Socrates attempted to lead Euthyphro in a fourth attempt at defining "holiness": Holiness is that part of justice that concerns the tending the gods. It only remained to define what sort of tendance was proper to the gods. However, Socrates dissents from the notion that this tendance could make the gods better. Checked in his fourth attempt, Euthyphro capitulates, returning to his previously rejected examples from the material world.

Unequal Exchange

... Now, however, it is necessary that the one asking follow the one being asked wherever he should lead. What then, once more, do you say that the holy and holiness are? Is it not some knowledge of sacrificing and praying?
Euthyphro: *I think so.*

Socrates now proposes that holiness is the science of sacrificing and praying. However, before doing so, he makes a rather cryptic remark about the one asking having to follow the direction of the one being asked. It is a strange inversion of the relationship between action and passion, one in which the passive is somehow the cause of the active. Or rather, one should recognize again the use of the middle voice. It is only true that "it is necessary that the one asking follow the one being asked" if "the one being asked" is also "the one causing to be asked." The use of the middle voice indicates that the Socratic maieutic is a meeting of souls, not bodies.

Socrates: *And is not then sacrificing the giving of gifts to the gods and is not praying a begging of the gods?*
Euthyphro: *Very much so, Socrates.*
Socrates: *Then according to this argument holiness would be a knowledge of begging and giving gifts.*

Euthyphro: *You understand beautifully, Socrates, what I was saying.*

Socrates: *For I am desirous, my friend, of your wisdom and put forth my mind to it, in order that whatever you say may not fall to the ground. But tell me, what is this service to the gods? Do you say that it is to beg from and give to them?*

Euthyphro: *I do.*

Socrates does not wish that Euthyphro's words should fall to the ground. In other words, he does not wish the argument to descend once again to the level of bodies. He also alludes to the myth of Daedalus and Icarus. Socrates, as Icarus, is following Euthyphro, who is a type of Daedalus. The result will not be long in coming.

Socrates: *Would not then begging rightly be asking them for those things which we are lacking?*

Euthyphro: *But what else?*

Socrates: *And in turn giving rightly would be to present in return those things which they happen to lack from us? For it would not in any way be artful that the one bringing gifts should give to someone those things of which he has no lack.*

Euthyphro: *Truly spoken, Socrates.*

Socrates: *Then holiness, Euthyphro, would be a mercantile art for gods and men between each other.*

Euthyphro: *'Mercantile' if it pleases you to name it thus.*

Socrates: *But it is no pleasure to me if it does not happen to be true. Now tell me, what benefit is there to the gods from the gifts that they receive from us? For the things that they give are clear to all. For we have nothing good which they do not in some way give. But how are they benefited by the things they receive from us? Or do we so far overreach them in bartering that we receive all good things from them, but they get nothing from us?*

If holiness is a science of sacrifice and prayer, determining what ought to be traded for worldly goods, it would indeed be "*a mercantile art for gods and men between each other.*" And, as pointed out several times, this is precisely the way the sophists and their students relate. However, an equivalence of value can only hold at the corporeal level, for there is an asymmetry between what the gods give to man and what man returns. There is no proportion, let alone equality, between the spiritual goods that the gods communicate to man and the material sacrifices returned by man to the gods. Equality in division is a property of the material and the even. The spiritual and odd implies an inequality of division. So, it is true that men receive all good things from the gods, but return little in value, from which it may be deduced that there is no genuine barter taking place. This distinction is preserved to this day in the notion of an *honorarium* given in return for lecturing, implying that there is no proportion between the benefit conferred and the remuneration received.

The stranger in *Statesman* points out the servile nature of the popular religion regarding both prophecy, in which Euthyphro claims a great share, and sacrifice:

> **Stranger:** Yet let us come to closer quarters with those who have not yet been put to the touchstone. There are those who have a share in a servant's knowledge concerning prophecy. For they are by custom the interpreters of the gods to men.
>
> **Young Socrates:** Yes.
>
> **Stranger:** And then also the class of priests, as custom affirms, know how to give gifts from us to the gods by sacrificing, gifts according to their divine minds, and by prayers to beg for us from them the acquisition of good things. And these are perhaps both a portion of the servant's art. (*Statesman* 290c-d)

The meaning of Euthyphro's original advice to Socrates that he "*come to close quarters*" with his enemies is made manifest: He ought to put them to the touchstone, to determine whether they are genuine gold. In the case of the Athenian priests, their interpretations and sacrifices are merely the custom of the people, corresponding to the customary names given by them to the gods. This popular religion does not depend upon an understanding by the prophet or priest of the divine Ideas. It is therefore not inappropriate to call these prophets and priests "servants," as they really do not know the gods. On the other hand, the relationship of philosophers to the gods is that of friendship, not of servitude.

Euthyphro: But do you think, Socrates, that the gods are benefited by these things they receive from us?

Socrates: But whatever would these be, Euthyphro, the gifts from us to the gods?

Euthyphro: What else would it be than honor and recognition and, what I was just saying, gratitude?

Socrates: Is the holy then, Euthyphro, that which is grateful to the gods, but not that which is beneficial or beloved of the gods?

Euthyphro: I for my part think that it is beloved more than anything.

Socrates: Then, it would seem that the holy is again the thing beloved of the gods.

Euthyphro: Yes, above all else.

For Plato, while it is certainly appropriate to offer the gods (including in the wider sense the philosophers) honor, recognition, and gratitude, and while these may indeed be pleasing to them, it is far from clear that the gods would need such recognition.

Circular Motion

Socrates: *Saying these things, do you then wonder if your words appear not to remain still but to walk about, and will you allege as a cause myself, a Daedalus, of making them walk, while you are much more skillful than Daedalus and make them go about in a circle? Or do you not perceive that our argument has come round again to the same definition? For you remember, I suppose, that the holy and that which is god-beloved did not seem to us the same thing before, but different from each other. Or do you not remember?*

Euthyphro: *I do remember.*

If there were need of additional proof that Euthyphro is firmly ensconced within the world of bodies, it is that his arguments go about in circles. Socrates argues in *Phaedo* that this is precisely the characteristic of generation, for a linear motion would tend toward only one of two contraries and would cease when all of nature shared the same passion:

> For if things coming to be did not always revert to their opposites, each to the other, as if going about in a circle, but if generation were instead straight, away from the one and toward its contrary, neither turning back upon itself nor making a bend, you know that all things would end up with the same character and would be passive by the same passion and would cease to be generated. (*Phaedo* 72a-b)

Euthyphro is thinking wholly at the level of generation, not essence.

Socrates: *Do you not comprehend now that you say that the thing beloved of the gods is holy? But is this something god-beloved or not?*

Euthyphro: *It is the same.*

Socrates: *Then either we were not agreeing beautifully before or, if beautifully then, we are not proposing rightly now.*

Euthyphro: *It would seem so.*

Socrates: *Then we must investigate again what the holy is, since I shall not willingly shrink from it out of cowardice before I learn. Do not despise me, but, applying your mind, by every means, tell me the truth fully now. For you know, if in fact any man does, and just like Proteus you must not be released until you speak. For if you did not know clearly both the holy and the unholy it is impossible that you would ever attempt to prosecute for murder an old man, your father, for the sake of a manservant, but you would have feared the gods to take such a risk, lest you should do it wrongfully and be shamed before men. But now I know well that you think you know clearly the holy and the unholy. Speak then, Euthyphro, best of men, and do not hide away what you think.*

Socrates continues to beg Euthyphro to teach him about holiness, pointing out that he has thus far refused to do so. The ironic tone with which Plato endows Socrates is a condemnation of Euthyphro, and thus of Meletus. He reminds Euthyphro that to undertake such a prosecution as he is planning would be construed a grave impiety if he were in fact wrong about the nature of holiness. He should fear to be "*shamed*," the kind of fear that accompanies reverence for the gods, rather than the fear of bodily ills. This wholesome and pious fear is not to be found in Euthyphro.

Socrates also states his unflinching intention of getting to the bottom of the matter, with Euthyphro's help, and to this end he will hold on to him, as if he were Proteus, until he yields up what Socrates wishes to know. The mention of Proteus alludes to Homer's *Odyssey*, in which Menelaus must discover which of the gods is angry with him. He discovers what is required from "Eidothea, daughter of mighty Proteus, the old man of the sea" (*Odyssey* 4.365-366). He must question her father:

> There is wont to come hither the unerring old man of the sea, immortal Proteus of Egypt, who knows the depths of every sea, and is the servant of Poseidon. He, they say, is my father that begat me. (*Odyssey* 4.384-386)

She instructs Menelaus to seize Proteus as he rests, not allowing him to escape, no matter what bodily form he may assume. When Proteus has exhausted all his wiles, he will tell Menelaus precisely what he needs to know:

> Now so soon as you see him laid to rest, thereafter let your heart be filled with strength and courage, and do you hold him there despite his striving and struggling to escape. For try he will, and will assume all manner of shapes of all things that move upon the earth, and of water, and of wondrous blazing fire. Yet do ye hold him unflinchingly and grip him yet the more. But when at length of his own will he speaks and questions thee in that shape in which you saw him laid to rest, then, hero, stay thy might, and set the old man free, and ask him who of the gods is wroth with thee, and of thy return, how thou mayest go over the teeming deep. (*Odyssey* 4.414-424)

This figure of Proteus represents Euthyphro, who has assumed every form in his answers, and yet has remained pinned down by Socrates. It also signifies the dialectical method by which one must arrive at the Ideas. For Eidothea, meaning "divine idea," is the daughter of Proteus. It is only by passing through these twists and turns of argument that one rises to the very essences of things.

❧

The Flight of Euthyphro

❧

Euthyphro: Another time, Socrates. For I am now hastening somewhere, and it is time for me to depart.

Socrates: What a thing you are doing, companion! You have left me, casting me down from the great hope which I had that, having learned from you about both holy things and those that are not, I would be freed from Meletus's charge, showing to him that I have become wise from Euthyphro about divine matters, and that I no longer rashly improvise from ignorance, nor do I innovate concerning these same things, and above all that I shall live better the rest of my life.

Euthyphro now flies from Socrates, refusing to teach him, just as Meletus did: "But you fled from associating with me and teaching me, being unwilling to do so." (*Apology*, 26a) He is "*hastening.*" Unlike Socrates, he has no time for "*playing like children.*" As father to Socrates, just as Daedalus was father to Icarus, Euthyphro fashioned bodily contrivances to serve in place of those wings stimulated by the "effluence of beauty," wings which would have allowed him to rise into the intelligible order. Fixated upon bodies, with their mere action and passion, he took flight on wings that would not withstand the heights of speculation. Socrates, desirous of exploring the realm of the Ideas and eager to test the answers given by Euthyphro, has now shown these wings to be corporeal simulacra. In the brightness of the Ideas and warmth of the Good, these answers have come apart, leaving nothing to sustain Socrates, who falls as Icarus did in the retelling of the story by Ovid:

> [Daedalus] urged Icarus to follow, taught him his ruinous arts, flapped his own wings, and looked back upon the wings of his son. Someone, while catching fish with a quivering reed, or a shepherd resting on his staff or a plowman upon his plow-handles, would see them and, stupefied that both were able to travel through the air, believe them to be gods. And soon Juno's Samos had been left behind on the left side, and Delos and Paros. On the right was Lebinthos and Calymne, fertile with honey, when the boy began to rejoice in his daring flight and drawn by a desire for the heavens forsook his guide and made his journey higher. The nearness of the swift sun softened the fragrant wax, the bonds of his feathers, and the wax melted away. He flapped his naked arms and lacking oars he caught no winds, but his lips, crying out the name of his father, were received by the azure water, which drew from him its name. (Ovid, *Metamorphoses*, Book VIII, 215-230)

It is Euthyphro who has improvised in religion, acting out of ignorance of the very nature of holiness. He and, by extension, Meletus have fallen short of philosophy, showing themselves to have no divine kinship with Zeus, the god of Friendship:

Now, Zeus, the great ruler in heaven, driving a winged chariot, first sets forth, putting in order all things and bestowing care upon them. (*Phaedrus* 246e)

Like Oedipus, Meletus will be compelled to admit: "Mine was no knowledge from birds." (*Oedipus the King*, 399) His condemnation is best expressed by the prophet Teiresias:

You have your eyes but see not where you are
in sin, nor where you live, nor whom you live with.
Do you know who your parents are? Unknowing
you are an enemy to kith and kin
in death, beneath the earth, and in this life.
A deadly footed, double striking curse,
from father and mother both, shall drive you forth
out of this land, with darkness on your eyes,
that now have such straight vision.
(*Oedipus the King*, 413-419)

Diogenes Laertius, *Lives of the Eminent Philosophers*, Loeb Classical Library, Vol. 184, 185 (Cambridge: Harvard, 1925)

Plato, *Alcibiades II*, Loeb Classical Library, Vol. 201, (Cambridge: Harvard, 1927)

Plato, *Apology*, Loeb Classical Library, Vol. 36, (Cambridge: Harvard, 1914)

Plato, *Cratylus*, Loeb Classical Library, Vol. 167, (Cambridge: Harvard, 1926)

Plato, *Critias*, Loeb Classical Library, Vol. 234, (Cambridge: Harvard, 1929)

Plato, *Epistles*, Loeb Classical Library, Vol. 234, (Cambridge: Harvard, 1929)

Plato, *Euthyphro*, Loeb Classical Library, Vol. 36, (Cambridge: Harvard, 1914)

Plato, *Gorgias*, Loeb Classical Library, Vol. 166, (Cambridge: Harvard, 1925)

Plato, *Laws*, Loeb Classical Library, Vol. 187, 192 (Cambridge: Harvard, 1926)

Plato, *Meno*, Loeb Classical Library, Vol. 165, (Cambridge: Harvard, 1924)

Plato, *Parmenides*, Loeb Classical Library, Vol. 167, (Cambridge: Harvard, 1929)

Plato, *Phaedo*, Loeb Classical Library, Vol. 36, (Cambridge: Harvard, 1914)

Plato, *Phaedrus*, Loeb Classical Library, Vol. 36, (Cambridge: Harvard, 1914)

Plato, *Philebus*, Loeb Classical Library, Vol. 164, (Cambridge: Harvard, 1925)

Plato, *Protagoras*, Loeb Classical Library, Vol. 165, (Cambridge: Harvard, 1924)

Plato, *Republic I.-V.*, Loeb Classical Library, Vol. 237, (Cambridge: Harvard, 1930)

Plato, *Republic VI.-X.*, Loeb Classical Library, Vol. 276, (Cambridge: Harvard, 1935)

Plato, *Sophist*, Loeb Classical Library, Vol. 123, (Cambridge: Harvard, 1921)

Plato, *Statesman*, Loeb Classical Library, Vol. 164, (Cambridge: Harvard, 1925)

Plato, *Symposium*, Loeb Classical Library, Vol. 166, (Cambridge: Harvard, 1925)

Plato, *Theaetetus*, Loeb Classical Library, Vol. 123, (Cambridge: Harvard, 1921)

Plato, *Timaeus*, Loeb Classical Library, Vol. 234, (Cambridge: Harvard, 1929)

Sextus Empiricus, *Against the Physicists*, Loeb Classical Library, Vol. 311, (Cambridge: Harvard, 1935)

Latin Texts Cited (Translated by Author)

Ovid, *Metamorphoses*, Loeb Classical Library, Vol. 42, (Cambridge: Harvard, 1977)

English Translations Cited

Anonymous, *Homeric Hymns: To Pythian Apollo*, translated by Hugh Evelyn-White, Loeb Classical Library, Vol. 57, (London: William Heinemann, 1914)

Hesiod, *Theogony*, translated by Hugh Evelyn-White, Loeb Classical Library, Vol. 57, (London: William Heinemann, 1914)

Homer, *Odyssey*, translated by A. T. Murray, Loeb Classical Library, Vol. 104, 105 (Cambridge: Harvard, 1919)

Sophocles, *Oedipus the King*, translated by David Grene, (Chicago: University of Chicago Press, 1942)

End Notes

[1] *Oxford Classical Dictionary*, 3rd Edition, "archontes," p. 150, (Oxford: Oxford Univ. Press, 1996)
[2] *Ibid. 1*, "law and procedure, Athenian, 3.," p. 826
[3] *Ibid. 1*, "Adonis," p. 12
[4] *Ibid. 1*, "prytaneion," pp. 1268-1269

www.ingramcontent.com/pod-product-compliance
Lightning Source LLC
Chambersburg PA
CBHW081927120726
47997CB00010B/3072